# HAIL MARY, HOLY BIBLE

# Hail Mary, Holy Bible

## Sacred Scripture and the Mysteries of the Rosary

Clifford M. Yeary

**LITURGICAL PRESS**

Collegeville, Minnesota

www.litpress.org

*Nihil Obstat:* Reverend Robert Harren, *Censor deputatus*
*Imprimatur:* ✠ Most Reverend Donald J. Kettler, J.C.L.,
  Bishop of Saint Cloud, Minnesota, November 23, 2016.

Cover design by Ann Blattner. Photo courtesy of Thinkstock by Getty Images.

| 1 | 2 | 3 | 4 | 5 | 6 | 7 | 8 | 9 |
|---|---|---|---|---|---|---|---|---|

**Library of Congress Cataloging-in-Publication Data**

Names: Yeary, Clifford M., author.
Title: Hail Mary, Holy Bible : sacred scripture and the mysteries of the
   Rosary / Clifford M. Yeary.
Description: Collegeville, Minnesota : Liturgical Press, 2017.
Identifiers: LCCN 2017017968 (print) | LCCN 2016052551 (ebook) | ISBN
   9780814636176 (ebook) | ISBN 9780814636169
Subjects: LCSH: Mysteries of the Rosary. | Jesus Christ—Biography. | Mary,
   Blessed Virgin, Saint—Biography. | Rosary. | Catholic Church—Doctrines.
Classification: LCC BT303 (print) | LCC BT303 .Y43 2017 (ebook) | DDC
   242/.74—dc23
LC record available at https://lccn.loc.gov/2017017968

With great affection and appreciation
this book is dedicated
to my colleagues at Little Rock Scripture Study:
Lilly Hess, Susan McCarthy, RDC, Catherine Upchurch,
and Nancy Lee Walters

# Contents

# *Preface*

One very significant blessing I received in writing this book came when I was writing the chapter on the sorrowful mysteries (chap. 3). It was just before Holy Week. I hadn't made any earth-shattering commitments to reform my life this last Lent. In fact, I've always wanted to rush through Lent and dive into Easter without getting scarred from the burdens of doing penance. But this Lent became different. While researching, reflecting, and writing about Jesus' agony in the garden, the scourging at the pillar, the crowning with thorns, the carrying of the cross, and, finally, the crucifixion, I discovered myself being there in the event. This is what the Jesuits have always praised about Ignatian reflection on Scripture. You don't just think about the words; you let the words construct the reality and draw you in as a witness to the sacred event. My great blessing in this was to take to heart what is so often said in religious circles, "There is no Easter without a Good Friday."

Sometime in the early 70s, when I was an Old Testament major in an evangelical university, a professor warned us that there was always a danger that one could become too familiar with Scripture, that one could become so certain of one's own scholarship that what you wrote, said, and taught about the Bible could squeeze God out of the Bible and end up being all about your own brilliant understanding. Since 2002 I have been blessed to serve as a writer and editor on staff with Little Rock Scripture Study. I am in my sixties and hope to retire before too long, but my years here have meant immersing myself in Scripture. Doing so as part of Little Rock Scripture Study has, I say hopefully, avoided the pitfall that professor warned against.

This is due in large part because of our director, Catherine "Cackie" Upchurch. Under her leadership Little Rock Scripture Study never forgets that it is a ministry of God's word. It exists because God's faithful have a hunger for God's word. They want to study Scripture with understanding, but they also want and need to be fed spiritually. Cackie has always kept our focus on being a ministry that both informs and nourishes, and if we are to do our jobs, we have to be not just learning, but growing in faith ourselves, continually being washed, as Paul says, by the water of the word (Eph 5:26). We are a small staff and everyone's efforts are essential. Without Lilllan Hess, Susan McCarthy, RDC, and Nancy Lee Walters my own job wouldn't get done. I am blessed to have them as colleagues and friends.

On top of everything else, though, I want to thank Cackie Upchurch for her superior skills as an editor, for all the sorry stuff she didn't let me say, and for all the good things she helped me say.

Finally, I want to give thanks to Liturgical Press. They are our partners in publication and everything they do exudes quality and professionalism and they all have my highest personal regard.

# Introduction

> Blessed are you who believed that what was spoken to you by the
> Lord would be fulfilled.
>
> —Luke 1:45

The closing words of Elizabeth's greeting to Mary at the visitation call out to us to contemplate the power of God's word spoken to us. In the pages ahead, we will explore the Sacred Scriptures that recount, or touch on, the four most common mysteries associated with the rosary: the Joyful Mysteries, the Mysteries of Light, the Sorrowful Mysteries, and the Glorious Mysteries.

Before we enter those mysteries, however, it might be best to consider why they are called mysteries. These mysteries are unlike those with which we are probably most familiar. These mysteries are not "whodunits." Indeed, the mysteries of the rosary are mysteries precisely because we are told who did it. They are mysteries because God is the principal actor, the person who is at the center of the story and yet also the author of the story, the one who sets the plot and brings the story to its fulfillment. God's presence in these mysteries, felt or unfelt, sought or rejected, is always beyond anyone's physical senses, thus the mystery of it all.

There is also the mystery that takes place in encountering Sacred Scripture. The Scriptures associated with the rosary do more than just recount sacred stories. They are the word of God, which is always a living word, a word intended and directed to transform our lives. There is no more powerful way to pray the rosary than to pray it while hearing and speaking Sacred Scripture as part of our prayerful contemplation.

The prophet referred to by scholars as Third Isaiah proclaimed God's word to the people of Judah at a time when they were struggling to find hope in God's promises, uncertain as to whether they would ever be fulfilled:

> "[J]ust as from the heavens
>    the rain and snow come down
> And do not return there
>    till they have watered the earth,
>    making it fertile and fruitful,
> Giving seed to the one who sows
>    and bread to the one who eats,
> So shall my word be
>    that goes forth from my mouth;
> It shall not return to me empty,
>    but shall do what pleases me,
>    achieving the end for which I sent it. (Isa 55:10-11)

The word of God, planted as a seed within human hearts, may wait not just years, or decades, but even generations before bearing fruit. A message from a prophet would be heard first in a specific context, at a specific time, in a specific place. In order to help us understand a prophet's message, those scholars responsible for interpreting Scripture do a lot of research into the time, place, and situation of those who first received the prophet's message. But messages don't just lay dormant once uttered, especially prophetic messages. Once people hear a message from someone they believe to be a prophet of God, they will keep the message alive and carry it with them. With both heart and mind they will ponder it, wondering always if they have fully understood it. This is true especially for a message of hope. Most of the time, most people live in hope of something better.

The children of Abraham were people of hope, but also people who had had their hopes dashed many times and yet never failed to trust in the words of hope planted in their hearts by the prophets. When the word of God takes root in the human heart, the word itself takes on a new context; it grows and flourishes in a new time and is carried into new places and new situations. Elizabeth and her kinswoman Mary met each other, greeted each other, swept up in that prophetic hope, in the ultimate hope, of a Messiah who would fulfill all the divine promises to Israel.

In praying the rosary while opening our hearts and minds to the word of God we inevitably encounter God incarnate in Christ Jesus. We also encounter Mary. Mary is the great role model for all Christians because of her response to the word of God. Mary is blessed because she believes that the word of the Lord spoken to her will be fulfilled even when it takes her life in directions she never contemplated. There is no doubting that God had a plan for her life; she was chosen to bear the Son of God. Could she possibly have imagined how her people, Israel, would respond to her son with both joyous acceptance and vile rejection? Their response to Jesus would have dire implications for her own life. It would eventually be a sword that would pierce her heart (Luke 2:35). Mary's example to us, however, is that she took all these things and reflected on them in her heart (Luke 2:19, 51).

One stunning image of Mary that grew over time was to see her as a new burning bush. When God first revealed himself to Moses, he did so by speaking to him from a bush at the foot of Mount Horeb (Sinai). The bush was brilliantly aflame and yet the fire did not consume it, allowing the bush, a created thing, to be something through which the Creator could reveal himself. Knowing that the eternal Word of God became incarnate in the womb of the Virgin Mary led early mystical theologians into understanding that Mary, throughout her pregnancy, was very much like the burning bush, a creature in whom the uncontainable God was contained, yet without being consumed. For centuries now, one of the focal icons in St. Catherine's Monastery at Mount Sinai, Egypt, is an icon of Mary as the burning bush.

I offer this commentary on the Sacred Scriptures associated with the mysteries of the rosary as an invitation to imitate Mary in taking the Word of God to heart, pondering it deeply, carrying it into our own circumstances, and allowing it to set our own hearts aflame, to ultimately allowing us to be witnesses to the world of God's merciful presence.

# CHAPTER I

# The Joyful Mysteries

## THE FIRST JOYFUL MYSTERY

### The Annunciation

*Luke 1:26-38*

[26]In the sixth month, the angel Gabriel was sent from God to a town of Galilee called Nazareth, [27]to a virgin betrothed to a man named Joseph, of the house of David, and the virgin's name was Mary. [28]And coming to her, he said, "Hail, favored one! The Lord is with you." [29]But she was greatly troubled at what was said and pondered what sort of greeting this might be. [30]Then the angel said to her, "Do not be afraid, Mary, for you have found favor with God. [31]Behold, you will conceive in your womb and bear a son, and you shall name him Jesus. [32]He will be great and will be called Son of the Most High, and the Lord God will give him the throne of David his father, [33]and he will rule over the house of Jacob forever, and of his kingdom there will be no end." [34]But Mary said to the angel, "How can this be, since I have no relations with a man?" [35]And the angel said to her in reply, "The holy Spirit will come upon you, and the power of the Most High will overshadow you. Therefore the child to be born will be called holy, the Son of God. [36]And behold, Elizabeth, your relative, has also conceived a son in her old age, and this is the sixth month for her who was called barren; [37]for nothing will be impossible for God." [38]Mary said, "Behold, I am the handmaid of the Lord. May it be done to me according to your word." Then the angel departed from her.

Hidden in Luke's straightforward reporting of the angel Gabriel's dutiful delivery of his special message to Mary is the stark contrast between the messenger and the recipient. Gabriel is not simply sent *by* God, but he is sent *from* God. This is the Gabriel who revealed himself to Zechariah in announcing the birth of John the Baptist. Gabriel's home in the universe is the immediate presence of God (Luke 1:19), and yet God sends this most privileged of beings to a tiny village (archaeological data suggests a population of under 150) to address a message to a young woman, who, having not yet married, has virtually no status even in this remote village of Israel—a foreign-occupied land that has lost status as a nation in its own right. With utter simplicity and brevity Luke leads us to this most unassuming stage for a message proclaiming the most important event since the creation of the universe.

Gabriel's salutation of the young, seemingly insignificant Mary elevates her status beyond anything she could possibly comprehend at the time. Thousands of years later, faithful believers around the world will prayerfully repeat Gabriel's greeting, sometimes in joy, at others in sorrow, praying also for enlightenment or hoping for a share in glory: "Hail, Mary, full of grace, the Lord is with you; blessed are you among women."

Mary was greatly troubled by the greeting and pondered its nature (1:28). In Judges 13:2-5, an angel of the Lord's appearance is described as that of a fearsome man. Not only would Mary be frightened, but her humility might even have made her suspicious: Why would this person, whoever or whatever it is, announce its presence by proclaiming that she is favored? Had anything in her life previous to this indicated that she was favored? And if she recognized this presence as a heavenly being, wouldn't it make his claim all the more baffling?

This tells us what a skillful writer Luke is, for in such very few words he leads us to understand that Mary is already unsettled by the greeting. How can she possibly be able to simply accept what the angel is going to tell her next? But Luke has also introduced us to a characteristic of Mary that he will continue to emphasize. Mary ponders Gabriel's greeting and Mary will continue to ponder throughout her life because of the events that will follow like aftershocks from the earthquake initiated in the angel's greeting.

The angel knows he has frightened her, and tells her not to be afraid. This is one of the most common phrases of reassurance found in the Bible. Because the reassurance is so common, we can be fairly certain that being frightened is the most common response to an encounter with the divine. Gabriel also gives her a specific reason for not being afraid. Having first hailed her as being favored, he now tells her the source of her favor: "[Y]ou have found favor with God" (1:30).

But nothing could be more baffling than how God proposes to show favor to Mary. She is to become pregnant and to bear a son she is to name Jesus, which means "Yah saves" (Yah is a shortened version of Yahweh, the name for God revealed to Moses through the burning bush [Exod 3:14-15]). Gabriel then quickly explains how great a favor this is by informing her of how great this son of hers will be. He will be called "God's Son" and he will inherit the throne of his ancestor David, but under her child's rule the kingdom will last forever.

Mary was probably among those Jews awaiting a messiah who would bring about the prophetic promises made concerning the royal house of David. The prophet Nathan assured David, "Your house and your kingdom are firm forever before me; your throne shall be firmly established forever" (2 Sam 7:16). Walter Brueggemann, one of the most prominent Old Testament scholars of our time, informs us that the subsequent kings of Judah, as descendants of David, foolishly used this divine promise of unwavering loyalty to assure themselves that they could manage their realm without regard for justice or faithfulness.

The royal line of David never had an heir to reign as king after the Babylonians destroyed Jerusalem in 587 BC. This left those who had faith in the prophetic promises to reassess what the promise meant. While they were in exile in Babylon, God instilled a new hope in the people through the prophet Ezekiel: "Say to them: Thus says the Lord GOD: I will soon take the Israelites from among the nations to which they have gone and gather them from all around to bring them back to their land. . . . They shall live on the land I gave to Jacob my servant, the land where their ancestors lived; they shall live on it always, they, their children, and their children's children, with David my servant as their prince forever" (Ezek 37:21, 25).

When Gabriel appeared to the Virgin Mary, the people had waited nearly six hundred years for a fulfillment of any prophecy concerning the reestablishment of the house of David providing a king over God's people. That the angel is identified as Gabriel is significant in this respect as well. Gabriel is the angel that reveals a vision of the messianic age to Daniel (Dan 8:16-17).

Being told that she will bring the Messiah into the world would seem to be the most startling thing any Jewish woman of the time could possibly hear, but however amazed Mary might be at the prospect, she has reason to wonder even more at its possibility. "How can this be, since I have no relations with a man?" she asks (1:34).

Long before Luke or Matthew provided accounts of Mary's virginal conception of Jesus, Paul made the first known mention of Jesus' birth in his letter to the Galatians (4:4-5): "[W]hen the fullness of time had come, God sent his Son, born of a woman, born under the law, to ransom those under the law, so that we might receive adoption." Paul makes no mention of Mary by name or any reference to her virginity. It is interesting that Paul makes no claim concerning Jesus' father, but it still raises the question, Why was Luke careful to inform his readers (literally "Theophilus," see 1:1-3) that Jesus was conceived through a virgin?

Luke's reasoning is found in Gabriel's response to Mary's question ("How can this be"): "The holy Spirit will come upon you, and the power of the Most High will overshadow you. Therefore the child to be born will be called holy, the Son of God." Jesus is not just the Son of God by adoption, but he literally had God as his father. But the matter of adoption is still important—the matter of our adoption. Jesus uniquely has God as his father, but he is also our brother and not just because he shares our human nature. Jesus has brought about our adoption as sons of the same father: we too have God as our father.

John tells us of Jesus' unique relationship with God by stressing that the eternal Word of the Father became one of us, fully human, in Jesus Christ. And his coming among us as one of us brings to us the possibility of being reborn as daughters and sons of God:

> He came to what was his own,
>   but his own people did not accept him.
> But to those who did accept him he gave power to become children of God, to those who believe in his name, who were born not by natural generation nor by human choice nor by a man's decision but of God. (John 1:11-13)

John does not use the word adoption, perhaps because he wants us to understand that our acceptance of Jesus, our belief "in his name," has made us children of God in the fullest possible sense. We are born again as children of God. His description of how that birth comes about is very much what Luke (and Matthew) tells us in proclaiming Mary's virginal conception and the birth of Jesus: he was born, "not by natural generation nor by human choice nor by a man's decision but of God."

We should be as astonished and bewildered by John's message to us as Mary was of Gabriel's.

Gabriel offers Mary a sign to authenticate what he has told her. Her kinswoman, Elizabeth, is also to have a child, she who, like Sarah long before her, is far too old to bear a child. Learning this, Mary believes and accepts her role in salvation history—"May it be done to me according to your word"—a role that will leave her constantly pondering, what can this mean?

## THE SECOND JOYFUL MYSTERY
### The Visitation
*Luke 1:36-37, 39-56*

[36]And behold, Elizabeth, your relative, has also conceived a son in her old age, and this is the sixth month for her who was called barren; [37]for nothing will be impossible for God." . . . [39]During those days Mary set out and traveled to the hill country in haste to a town of Judah, [40]where she entered the house of Zechariah and greeted Elizabeth. [41]When Elizabeth heard Mary's greeting, the infant leaped in her womb, and Elizabeth, filled with the holy Spirit, [42]cried out in a loud voice and said, "Most blessed are you among women, and blessed is the fruit of your womb. [43]And how does this happen to me, that the mother of my Lord should come to me? [44]For at the moment the sound of your greeting reached my ears, the infant in my womb leaped for joy. [45]Blessed are you who believed that what was spoken to you by the Lord would be fulfilled."

[46]And Mary said:
"My soul proclaims the greatness of the Lord;
   [47]my spirit rejoices in God my savior.
[48]For he has looked upon his handmaid's lowliness;
   behold, from now on will all ages call me blessed.
[49]The Mighty One has done great things for me,
   and holy is his name.
[50]His mercy is from age to age
   to those who fear him.
[51]He has shown might with his arm,
   dispersed the arrogant of mind and heart.
[52]He has thrown down the rulers from their thrones
   but lifted up the lowly.

<sup>53</sup>The hungry he has filled with good things;
    the rich he has sent away empty.
<sup>54</sup>He has helped Israel his servant,
    remembering his mercy,
<sup>55</sup>according to his promise to our fathers,
    to Abraham and to his descendants forever."

<sup>56</sup>Mary remained with her about three months and then returned to her home.

Mary was given a sign. When she asked the angel Gabriel how it could be that she would bear a son as a virgin, he told her that her relative, Elizabeth, had conceived in her old age. If that could be true, then truly her own pregnancy as a virgin was not a thing too difficult for God.

And so Mary set out in haste. But the reasons for her haste were not simply to verify the angel's words. If she were just wondering if the angel's words were true—if it could really be possible that Elizabeth, in her old age, had actually become pregnant—she might have simply waited around until the news reached her at home in Nazareth. The news would be momentous and would certainly reach her in time. Tradition holds that Elizabeth and Zechariah lived in a small village five miles outside of Jerusalem, known as Ein Karem (English spellings vary). From Mary's home in Nazareth to Ein Karem it was a distance of just under ninety miles. It would have been quite a journey, lasting several days, if not a week, on foot. That Mary set out in haste better demonstrates her enthusiasm at learning of Elizabeth's pregnancy than it would a desire to verify the angel's words. Making haste in such a journey reveals Mary's determination and purposefulness. Haste, in this case, does not suggest she set out unprepared or on a whim. She was a very young Jewish woman in an extremely patriarchal culture. Her pregnancy probably occurred near her transition from girl to woman and she would not, could not, set out on such a journey on her own. She would have to be chaperoned by an adult male relative, and that would require a family discussion at the very least, but Luke tells us nothing about that. Such details lie outside Luke's purpose in describing Mary's visitation of Elizabeth.

It is important for Luke to provide the warm details of the visitation, including Elizabeth's greeting, the joyful response of John within her womb, and Mary's ecstatic prayer (the *Magnificat*), because they all point to Jesus' unparalleled stature. As great as John the Baptist will be, his role in salvation history is to point the way to Christ. This is the message Luke intends to convey in proclaiming this marvelous event to us.

Upon entering "the house of Zechariah" Mary greeted Elizabeth and a great rejoicing occurs. Elizabeth, six months pregnant with John, knows immediately that Mary too is expecting a child. She knows because even in the womb John cannot withhold his joy at being in the presence of the one to whom he will bear witness in the ultimate fulfillment of his own prophetic calling. Mary, Elizabeth, and John are three people whom Christians will count as the most privileged people on earth at this point, for they and they alone know whose presence they are in, but their exultation springs from their humility.

"[H]ow does this happen to me," asks Elizabeth, "that the mother of my Lord should come to me?" And Mary's answer to that question is equally humble. "[M]y spirit rejoices in God my savior. / For he has looked upon his handmaid's lowliness." When Mary proclaims, "behold, from now on will all ages call me blessed," she does so in all humility:

> "My soul proclaims the greatness of the Lord;
>  my spirit rejoices in God my savior.
> For he has looked upon his handmaid's lowliness."

In looking upon his handmaid's lowliness, God has forever exalted her: "behold, from now on will all ages call me blessed."

The first to call her blessed was Elizabeth: "Most blessed are you among women, and blessed is the fruit of your womb." Elizabeth's blessing is, of course, at the heart of the prayer we know as "the Hail Mary." This makes Elizabeth's original blessing of Mary the source of those countless blessings fulfilling Mary's prophetic claim that "from now on will all ages call me blessed."

The *Magnificat* (Luke 1:46-55) is proclaimed only during the Liturgy of the Word during Mass on August 15 (solemnity of the Assumption) and on December 22 (except when that is the 4th Sunday of Advent). In the Liturgy of the Hours—the official prayer of the church and the duty of all ordained and vowed religious—evening prayer always includes the *Magnificat*. As a literary form it is called a canticle. In the Bible a canticle is a hymn of praise found outside the book of Psalms. There are many in the Old Testament. The first one is found in Exodus and is commonly called the Song of Moses (Exod 15:1-9). Many scholars consider it one of the oldest texts found in the Bible.

The *Magnificat* is most similar to the Prayer of Hannah (1 Sam 2:1-10). The similarity between Hannah's canticle and the *Magnificat* is more than just in their content. The similarity between the two is felt even more in their context. Hannah, Mary, and Elizabeth are all associated with the birth of sons that came into the world only through God's miraculous intervention.

Hannah was the mother of the prophet Samuel, who would anoint the first two kings of Israel, Saul and David. Hannah was one of two wives of a Levitical priest named Elkanah. His other wife bore children and Hannah had borne none, but while praying in desperation she promised the Lord that if she were to bear a son, she would surrender him, after he was weaned, to a lifetime of dedicated service to God as a Nazarite—those who, like John the Baptist, refused all alcoholic beverages and never cut their hair.

In their canticles, both Hannah and Mary rejoice in God's merciful interventions, interventions that bring about great reversals in human affairs. For Luke this is captured in Jesus' proclamation of the kingdom of God. Jesus makes God's reign visible and present through his teaching, healing, and forgiving, bringing about a merciful reversal in typical human affairs, which always favor the powerful over the weak. Notice the reversals that Hannah praises God for bringing about in her canticle:

> "The bows of the mighty are broken,
>     while the tottering gird on strength.
> The well-fed hire themselves out for bread,
>     while the hungry no longer have to toil.
> The barren wife bears seven sons,
>     while the mother of many languishes." (1 Sam 2:4-5)

Hannah proclaims the power of God to reverse the historical trends that favor those who take and ignore only the needs of the poor, the humble, and the meek. Her proclamation is mirrored in the *Magnificat*:

> "He has shown might with his arm,
>     dispersed the arrogant of mind and heart.
> He has thrown down the rulers from their thrones
>     but lifted up the lowly.
> The hungry he has filled with good things;
>     the rich he has sent away empty." (Luke 1:51-53)

Canticles and psalms are a rich core tradition in biblical literature. They are such an integral part of Israel's prayer life that it should come as no surprise that biblical scholars are mostly agreed that the *Magnificat* may not have originated with Mary. It is quite likely to have been handed down in one or more versions from both Jewish and Christian sources. Luke would have set it down in writing because it ideally reflected Mary's spirituality. If she did not pray it verbatim, she certainly prayed it in essence.

At the heart of the visitation is a universal human story that proclaims the joy of kinship, the welcoming of new life—even in seemingly impossible circumstances—and the hopeful prayer that the joys and bounty of life can be shared by everyone and not just the rich and powerful.

In telling the story of the visitation, Luke reveals that he had a very specific theological purpose in the way he presented it. Its universal themes do not detract from his purpose. Instead, they help him fulfill his purpose. The humble of the earth, like these two humble women, help Luke to proclaim a truth essential to his gospel: John the Baptist's role in salvation history was to humble himself by bearing witness to the one who was greater than he. And Mary too, though she was to be called blessed throughout all time, received her blessing because of the child she was carrying in her womb.

## THE THIRD JOYFUL MYSTERY

### The Nativity

*Luke 2:1-20*

> [1]In those days a decree went out from Caesar Augustus that the whole world should be enrolled. [2]This was the first enrollment, when Quirinius was governor of Syria. [3]So all went to be enrolled, each to his own town. [4]And Joseph too went up from Galilee from the town of Nazareth to Judea, to the city of David that is called Bethlehem, because he was of the house and family of David, [5]to be enrolled with Mary, his betrothed, who was with child. [6]While they were there, the time came for her to have her child, [7]and she gave birth to her first-born son. She wrapped him in swaddling clothes and laid him in a manger, because there was no room for them in the inn.
>
> [8]Now there were shepherds in that region living in the fields and keeping the night watch over their flock. [9]The angel of the Lord appeared to them and the glory of the Lord shone around them, and they were struck with great fear. [10]The angel said to them, "Do not be afraid; for behold, I proclaim to you good news of great joy that

will be for all the people. ¹¹For today in the city of David a savior
has been born for you who is Messiah and Lord. ¹²And this will be a
sign for you: you will find an infant wrapped in swaddling clothes
and lying in a manger." ¹³And suddenly there was a multitude of the
heavenly host with the angel, praising God and saying:

> ¹⁴"Glory to God in the highest
>     and on earth peace to those on whom his favor rests."

¹⁵When the angels went away from them to heaven, the shepherds
said to one another, "Let us go, then, to Bethlehem to see this thing
that has taken place, which the Lord has made known to us." ¹⁶So
they went in haste and found Mary and Joseph, and the infant lying
in the manger. ¹⁷When they saw this, they made known the message that had been told them about this child. ¹⁸All who heard it
were amazed by what had been told them by the shepherds. ¹⁹And
Mary kept all these things, reflecting on them in her heart. ²⁰Then
the shepherds returned, glorifying and praising God for all they had
heard and seen, just as it had been told to them.

Only Matthew and Luke give us accounts of Jesus' nativity. Because
of the rosary's intimate association with Mary, because Matthew's nativity account is more concerned with Joseph than with Mary, it is Luke's
account that provides the basis for this scriptural examination of the
third joyful mystery of the rosary. Nevertheless, because "the Christmas
story" we are told and sing about from childhood is usually an amalgam
of the two accounts, there is good reason to provide a table that outlines
both the parallels and contrasts between Matthew and Luke's separate
accounts of both the annunciation and nativity (see appendix).

Luke tells us that Mary and Joseph were required to travel to Bethlehem from Nazareth because Joseph had to register there as a member
of the tribe of Judah during the reign of the Roman Emperor Augustus,
while Quirinius was governor of Syria. Biblical scholars and historians
note that there seems to be no evidence of a Roman census at that time.

To get past this problem, let's consider an important theological truth
Luke's assertion makes. At the very least, we have to assume that Luke
is attempting to show that the birth of Jesus Christ is of great historical
consequence. From Luke's perspective, placing the birth of Christ in a
time and place firmly under the control of the Roman Empire and its
toadies is a way of demonstrating how God's activity in the world up-
stages any show of power or authority that earthly rulers can exert. The
birth of Jesus, the one of whom Gabriel told Mary "he will rule over the

house of Jacob forever, and of his kingdom there will be no end" (1:33), occurs without any sign of earthly pomp or celebration. He is born in a stable and placed in a manger because the world had no room for him. When Caesar Augustus took his throne, it was acclaimed as "good news," throughout the empire. The Good News of the salvation Jesus will bring to the world will be acclaimed long after Augustus dies; it will be spread with signs and wonders "to the ends of the earth" (Acts 1:8). The humble nature of Jesus' birth and its incredible importance to the world is a pointed example of the theme of the great reversal found in the previous comparison of Hannah's prayer with the *Magnificat*.

*Do we?*

Both Matthew and Luke are in agreement that Jesus was born in Bethlehem. Bethlehem was the birthplace of King David. Because of the prophetic promises made to David and his heirs ("Your house and your kingdom are firm forever before me; your throne shall be firmly established forever [2 Sam 7:16]), the hope for an ultimate heir to David's line was expected to come to power out of Bethlehem:

> But you, Bethlehem-Ephrathah
>    least among the clans of Judah,
> From you shall come forth for me
>    one who is to be ruler in Israel;
> Whose origin is from of old,
>    from ancient times. (Mic 5:1)

In announcing that Mary gave birth to her firstborn son (Luke 2:7), Luke isn't hinting that the Virgin Mary would have other children. He is, rather, preparing us for our next encounter with Christ in his gospel, which is also the next joyful mystery of the rosary: the presentation of the baby Jesus in the temple.

The angel of the Lord appears to some shepherds of the region. Earlier, Gabriel was identified as the angel of the Lord, but that doesn't mean there is only one angel of the Lord. As in Old Testament times, the distinction between the angel of the Lord and God is not always razor sharp, for along with the appearance of the angel the shepherds also witness "the glory of the Lord," which strikes great fear in them (2:8-9). Scripture is consistent in presenting us with the divine response to fear in the presence of the Almighty: "Do not be afraid."

The particular reason the angel gives for calming their fears is an early proclamation of the gospel, the Good News of Jesus Christ: A savior is born to us, a gift of great joy for all the people. The news is so wondrous that all the denizens of heaven, "the heavenly host," make their praise of God in the presence of the shepherds. Their words are embedded in the Gloria at the opening of the eucharistic liturgy, which is its own highest order of praise for God:

> "Glory to God in the highest
> and on earth peace to those on whom his favor rests."

While the appearance of the angelic host to the shepherds includes a clear proclamation of the Gospel, Luke's use of them should remind Christians of all succeeding generations that the Gospel belongs in a special way to the poor. When Jesus is born, only shepherds are told of his birth and only the shepherds seek him out. Shepherds were regarded as lowliest of the lowly in Israelite society. When shepherding was part of a family responsibility, rather than the job of hirelings, it was a job for the youngest in the family. As the youngest in his family, David had to be fetched from his shepherding duties when Samuel came looking for someone in Jesse's family to anoint as king (1 Sam 16:1-13). When it was a job for hirelings, it was a job given to young children, quite often girls.

In Matthew's account of the nativity, those who visit the newborn king may themselves be royalty, but at the very least, the magi are wealthy sages who are able to gain an audience with King Herod. In this way, and also with the gift of gold the magi bring, Matthew emphasizes Jesus' royalty. Luke truly regards Jesus as the Messiah, who is the promised king in the line of David, but in informing us of the divine proclamation of the Gospel to the shepherds, Luke once again tells us that Jesus has come to upset the old world order. The Gospel will raise up the poor and cast down the mighty.

Unlike the magi in Matthew's gospel, the shepherds are not given a star to lead them to the newborn Savior. They have only the angel's announcement that this Savior is lying in a manger somewhere in nearby Bethlehem, bundled inside a snug wrap. There were probably more than a few stables and mangers in Bethlehem. Any household of the time that could afford animals would typically have a stable on the ground floor of their house. The shepherds weren't told to look for an "inn," probably because the Greek term used for the traditional rendering as an "inn" more correctly simply refers to a guest room in a house. But inspiration can lead from within, and we know that the shepherds found them and told Mary and Joseph how the angels had announced the Good News and location of Jesus' birth (2:17).

*[handwritten marginal note: Contrast of shepherds and magi]*

Luke concludes his account of Jesus' birth by giving two examples of discipleship for us to emulate. The shepherds, unrestrained in their joy at finding Mary and Joseph, and the infant in the manger, just as the angel had told them, tell everyone about the message they were given about the child. Luke has cleverly worded this. It is not specifically the news that they had found the child that they report with joy; rather it is "the *message that had been told them about this child*" (2:17, emphasis added). The message is the Gospel, the Good News about the Christ. The shepherds, like all those who will later be touched by Jesus in some way, become evangelists, and Luke sets them up to be examples for us.

The second example of discipleship that Luke gives us is the infant's mother, Mary. Upon hearing the shepherds speak of the angel's message, "Mary kept all these things, reflecting on them in her heart." It is neither the first nor the last time Luke will tell of Mary's reflective nature (1:29; 2:19; 2:51). We are like Mary when we take God's word to heart, pondering what it can mean for us as disciples.

## THE FOURTH JOYFUL MYSTERY

### The Presentation

*Luke 2:21-38*

[21]When eight days were completed for his circumcision, he was named Jesus, the name given him by the angel before he was conceived in the womb.

[22]When the days were completed for their purification according to the law of Moses, they took him up to Jerusalem to present him to the Lord, [23]just as it is written in the law of the Lord, "Every male that opens the womb shall be consecrated to the Lord," [24]and to offer the sacrifice of "a pair of turtledoves or two young pigeons," in accordance with the dictate in the law of the Lord.

[25]Now there was a man in Jerusalem whose name was Simeon. This man was righteous and devout, awaiting the consolation of Israel, and the holy Spirit was upon him. [26]It had been revealed to him by the holy Spirit that he should not see death before he had seen the Messiah of the Lord. [27]He came in the Spirit into the temple; and when the parents brought in the child Jesus to perform the custom of the law in regard to him, [28]he took him into his arms and blessed God, saying:

[29]"Now, Master, you may let your servant go
in peace, according to your word,

³⁰for my eyes have seen your salvation,
  ³¹which you prepared in sight of all the peoples,
³²a light for revelation to the Gentiles,
  and glory for your people Israel."

³³The child's father and mother were amazed at what was said about him; ³⁴and Simeon blessed them and said to Mary his mother, "Behold, this child is destined for the fall and rise of many in Israel, and to be a sign that will be contradicted ³⁵(and you yourself a sword will pierce) so that the thoughts of many hearts may be revealed." ³⁶There was also a prophetess, Anna, the daughter of Phanuel, of the tribe of Asher. She was advanced in years, having lived seven years with her husband after her marriage, ³⁷and then as a widow until she was eighty-four. She never left the temple, but worshiped night and day with fasting and prayer. ³⁸And coming forward at that very time, she gave thanks to God and spoke about the child to all who were awaiting the redemption of Jerusalem.

When Luke wrote his gospel sometime after the Romans destroyed the Jewish temple in AD 70, Jewish religious authorities no longer recognized as Jews those who professed Jesus as their Messiah. Gentile believers already far outnumbered Jewish adherents to the messianic movement that was once called "the Way" (Acts 9:2; 18:25-26), and both were beginning to be grouped together as "Christians." A new religion had emerged out of Judaism. This posed a problem for Luke concerning God's faithfulness. From within his gospel and the book of Acts (which he also wrote) it is evident that he was determined to answer Gentiles who criticized Christian belief in Jesus as the Jewish Messiah on the grounds that Jesus had been rejected as the Messiah by his own people. Some critics of early Christianity appear to have suggested that the Christian God was fickle, abandoning one set of people to join himself to another.

Luke began his gospel by assuring his audience, whom he referred to as "Theophilus" (who might have been a theoretical figure representing an entire Christian community), that because of Luke's careful research he might "realize the certainty of the teachings" regarding Jesus that Theophilus had already received (see 1:1-4). Luke wanted to affirm that regardless of how few Jews were presently followers of Christ, from the very beginning of his life, Jesus had been received with great joy by devout Jews, and that Jesus himself had been raised in a holy and devout Jewish family who faithfully adhered to Jewish religious practices.

Luke's second book, Acts, records how the early church leaders, meeting in Jerusalem, resolved the first major crisis that threatened to split the church in two. Paul and others were admitting uncircumcised Gentiles to baptism and full membership in the Christian faith. Many other early Christian missionaries, both Jewish and Gentile, insisted that male circumcision was a required sign of anyone who claimed to be part of the messianic people. In Acts, Luke describes how the early church, inspired by the Holy Spirit, came to the conclusion that circumcision was not a requirement for Gentile Christians (Acts 15:1-29).

Luke, however, found it necessary in his gospel to demonstrate Jesus' own fidelity to the covenant God had made with the Jewish people. In their care of Jesus, Joseph and Mary were scrupulously faithful to the covenant God had made with Abraham and Moses and so they had Jesus circumcised eight days after his birth (see Lev 12:3).

Perhaps because Luke was writing for a Gentile audience, what Luke tells us about the presentation of the Lord does not tightly mirror what someone fully aware of Jewish practice during Jesus' lifetime would expect. First of all, it was not necessary to present a firstborn son at the temple. But that they did so at the temple underscores Joseph and Mary's devotion to the temple.

Luke also seems to suggest that both Joseph and Mary waited the required time (forty days) for their mutual purification before going to the temple: "When the days were completed for their purification according to the law of Moses, they took him up to Jerusalem to present him to the Lord" (2:22). According to Jewish law concerning a firstborn son only the mother was required to wait forty days before entering the temple area. What Luke tells us, however, is that they all, Joseph, Mary, and Jesus, went together to the temple to present Jesus to the Lord.

At the heart of the presentation of a firstborn male to Israel's God is a sacrifice that "redeems" the child. On the night of the exodus, when all the firstborn males of Egypt were taken by the Lord, the firstborn males of the Hebrews were spared because the blood of their Passover lambs had been sprinkled on their doorposts (Exod 12:21-27). The first commandment God gives Moses following the Passover is the requirement that all firstborn males be consecrated to the Lord (Exod 13:1). This meant that once consecrated to the Lord they belonged completely to God, and in order for the family to receive the child back into their care, the child had to be "redeemed" by offering a sacrifice.

There are only two types of animals that can be sacrificed for the child's redemption: those who can afford it must offer a lamb. The poor can offer birds—either two turtledoves or two pigeons (Lev 12:2-8). Once again we are reminded that Mary and Joseph are poor, members of the *anawim*, the most humble class in Israel. Yet, in their humble state, their righteousness and faithfulness shine forth.

With Simeon and Anna's encounters with the infant Jesus, our attention is drawn even closer to Luke's concern to show us that there were those faithful Israelites who, led by the Holy Spirit, recognized Jesus as the Messiah. Simeon, an old man who has spent his life hoping to see the fulfillment of God's promises to bring peace and comfort to Israel, praises God for revealing the answer to his greatest desire in life in the infant Jesus. But Simeon also sees that Jesus will bring about not only consolation for Israel, but discord as well. He warns Mary, "[T]his child is destined for the fall and rise of many in Israel, and to be a sign that will be contradicted" (2:34).

Simeon then tells Mary, almost as an aside, that controversy over Jesus will prove to rend her own heart in a near fatal manner: "[A]nd you yourself a sword will pierce" (2:35a). This is prophecy, of course, but not one to be understood literally. There is no account in Luke or any of our gospels that indicate that the crucified body of Jesus was ever placed in the arms of his mother, but Michelangelo's deeply moving *Pietà* surely expresses the pain of the metaphorical sword that Simeon promised would pierce her.

Simeon goes on to tell Mary that a reason for Jesus being a sign of contradiction in Israel is "so that the thoughts of many hearts may be revealed" (2:35b). Who we are in truth can be revealed by how we respond to Jesus and his teachings. Later in Luke, the adult Jesus will tell his followers much the same thing: "Do you think that I have come to establish peace on the earth? No, I tell you, but rather division. From now on a household of five will be divided, three against two and two against three" (12:51-52). Matthew marks the point even more sharply: "Do not think that I have come to bring peace upon the earth. I have come to bring not peace but the sword" (10:34).

While Simeon is not called a prophet, he does prophesy concerning Jesus' destiny. The elderly Anna, on the other hand, is designated as a prophet(ess), yet the apparent prophecy she receives is not revealed, except to say that she, too, somehow recognizes who Jesus is, gives thanks to God, and then proclaims what could be called an early stage of the Gospel that Luke is proclaiming "to all who were awaiting the redemption of Jerusalem" (2:38).

We should not miss the importance to Luke's narrative that both Simeon and Anna are elderly and noted for their devotion to God. Simeon is "righteous and devout," while Anna "never left the temple, but worshiped night and day with fasting and prayer." Their old age reminds us that there were those in Israel who had been hoping for the Messiah for a long time, and for those who could recognize in the infant that God had begun to fulfill the ancient promises to Israel, Jesus was already peace and consolation. Controversy over Jesus would create a storm from the moment Jesus took up his ministry to Israel, but for those who can see by faith who Jesus is, he is not only peace and consolation, but also the crowning joy of a fulfilled life.

## THE FIFTH JOYFUL MYSTERY
### Finding the Young Jesus in the Temple
*Luke 2:39-52*

[39]When they had fulfilled all the prescriptions of the law of the Lord, they returned to Galilee, to their own town of Nazareth. [40]The child grew and became strong, filled with wisdom; and the favor of God was upon him.
[41]Each year his parents went to Jerusalem for the feast of Passover, [42]and when he was twelve years old, they went up according to festival custom. [43]After they had completed its days, as they were returning, the boy Jesus remained behind in Jerusalem, but his parents did not know it. [44]Thinking that he was in the caravan, they journeyed for a day and looked for him among their relatives and acquaintances, [45]but not finding him, they returned to Jerusalem to look for him. [46]After three days they found him in the temple, sitting in the midst of the teachers, listening to them and asking them questions, [47]and all who heard him were astounded at his understanding and his answers. [48]When his parents saw him, they were astonished, and his mother said to him, "Son, why have you done this to us? Your father and I have been looking for you with great anxiety." [49]And he said to them, "Why were you looking for me? Did you not know that I must be in my Father's house?" [50]But they did not understand what he said to them. [51]He went down with them and came to Nazareth, and was obedient to them; and his mother kept all these things in her heart. [52]And Jesus advanced [in] wisdom and age and favor before God and man.

If it were not for Luke's account of Joseph and Mary finding the twelve-year-old Jesus in the temple, we would know nothing of what Jesus did or said as a child. At twelve, he is just on the verge of being considered a man. In later times, Jewish boys would make the transition from childhood to adulthood at thirteen through the ritual of becoming a "son of the law" (bar mitzvah). This was the age at which Jewish boys become accountable before God for their own actions (for girls, it is twelve).

Some have speculated that Luke's account of the finding in the temple actually describes Jesus' bar mitzvah, but we simply don't know if or when or how the equivalent of a bar mitzvah was celebrated in Jesus' day. According to noted Lukan scholar Joseph Fitzmyer, however, this scene does reveal what, in later Judaism, a bar mitzvah is supposed to demonstrate concerning a Jewish male who is entering the religious and moral responsibilities of adulthood. In being questioned by religious authorities in the temple, Jesus demonstrates that he is fully trained in the Torah and capable of fulfilling all the adult obligations of a faithful Jew.

Luke tells us that Joseph and Mary returned to Nazareth after the presentation in the temple. Of the twelve years between the time of their return and the finding of Jesus in the temple, we are told only that "[t]he child grew and became strong, filled with wisdom; and the favor of God was upon him" (2:40). This is important, though, because it tells us that Jesus grew and developed as a child. He enjoyed God's favor, he endeavored to learn what God wanted of him (he was filled with wisdom), and he developed physically. There are no hints of miraculous behavior or knowledge, but only exceptionally good behavior accompanied by the acquisition of wisdom. At this point he does not appear to be all that different from John the Baptist as a child, who "grew and became strong in spirit" (1:80).

We have always idealized the Holy Family. What better parents could there be than Joseph and Mary? Even the setting for this account reminds us that they are faithful servants of God, having dutifully journeyed to Jerusalem to celebrate the Passover "according to festival custom" (Luke 2:42, see also Deut 16:2). And yet the adolescent Jesus can stray from their care as they return from a journey to Jerusalem and his disappearance is not noticed for some time. Luke does not suggest there is any fault on their part, however. They were both thinking he was somewhere in the throng of returning pilgrims.

It would have been customary for Jewish pilgrims to travel together, in a "caravan," but probably not in mixed company when in a large group. The women and children would walk together and the men would accompany each other. And this may be the source of the problem. Is Jesus, at twelve, a young man or a child? Could Mary have thought he was with the men, and Joseph thought he was with the women? All Luke tells us is that they "looked for him among their relatives and acquaintances" (2:44). But that alone is a pleasant thought for reflection. Joseph and Mary and Jesus were not loners. They were sociable. They had friends and relatives and they naturally assumed that Jesus might choose to be in their company.

The more carefully readers recognize that point, the sharper they will feel Luke's primary message in this unique account concerning the boy/man Jesus. Who does Jesus want to be with, who is his preferred company: friends, relatives, or parents?

Desperate to find him once they realize they have lost him, they return to Jerusalem. It has been three days since they last saw him when they look for him in the temple. When we find the phrase "three days" associated with Jesus in the New Testament, we are probably never wrong in thinking that we are being either reminded of or told of Jesus' resurrection from the dead. Jesus has been lost to his family for three days, but on that third day he is found again.

Mary, his mother, would of course be very relieved. In fact, both Mary and Joseph are astonished, because Jesus is seated with the religious teachers in the temple, and they are exhibiting their own astonishment at both his answers and his understanding. But Luke tells us that Mary has also been put out by Jesus' behavior. What he has done is no way to treat his family. "[H]is mother said to him, 'Son, why have you done this to us? Your father and I have been looking for you with great anxiety'" (2:48). Jesus answers her question with two of his own, and they are the first words we are told that Jesus ever spoke: "Why were you looking for me? Did you not know that I must be in my Father's house?" (2:49).

It is the unstated answers to those questions that tell us why Luke wanted this account to appear in his gospel. In the first part of this account, Luke speaks freely of Mary and Joseph as being Jesus' parents, and Jesus' disappearance from their care becomes a great stress on them. When they find him in the temple, Mary once again reminds Jesus of his obligation to his parents, referring to Joseph and herself as "your father and I" (2:48).

Jesus' answer, his questions—"Why were you looking for me? Did you not know that I must be in my Father's house?" (2:49)—tells them something very difficult to grasp, that his true Father expects him to be engaged in the family business. "But they did not understand what he said to them" (2:50).

At the annunciation, we learned that the angel Gabriel informed Mary that her son would be called the "Son of the Most High" and "the Son of God" (1:32, 35), but it was not a lack of faith on Mary's part that she would have to struggle with what that meant for her and her relationship to her son. At Jesus' birth when the shepherds related their encounter with the heavenly host and the angel's message to them, we are told, "Mary kept all these things, reflecting on them in her heart" (2:19). What her son will say and do and experience in the world will require a lot of reflection, a lot of soul-searching, prayer, and faith. When the aged holy man Simeon warned her in that previous visit to the temple that her infant child would be a cause of great controversy, his parenthetical warning that she would experience the piercing of a sword was probably, in part, preparing her for the many moments like this one when her son's obedience to the Father would rend her heart.

Jesus' behavior in remaining behind in Jerusalem, leaving Joseph and Mary to worry and wonder what possibly could have become of him, was just the beginning of a growing tension. The biological bond between mother and child will prove insufficient for Jesus. Jesus will ultimately require a bond that arises from faith and the commitment that marks discipleship. After his baptism, when Jesus was fully dedicated to his mission of proclaiming the kingdom of God, Mary and his family (those who were regarded as his brothers) wanted to come to him, but the crowds around Jesus were too large and they couldn't get near. His family sent word through the crowd: "He was told, 'Your mother and your brothers are standing outside and they wish to see you.'" Jesus' response was to redefine his family as those who take to heart his words and put them into action: "My mother and my brothers are those who hear the word of God and act on it" (Luke 8:19-21).

After finding the young Jesus in the temple, Mary was troubled, but she didn't doubt; instead, she "kept all these things in her heart" (2:51). This is what completes Mary's motherhood. She not only gave Jesus birth, she not only raised and cared for him, but from the very beginning she pondered his presence in the world and now, his words and deeds. Others have seen, heard, and been amazed, but his mother became our Lord's first disciple.

# CHAPTER 2

# The Mysteries of Light

## THE FIRST MYSTERY OF LIGHT
### The Baptism of the Lord
*Matthew 3:1-6; 13-17*

¹In those days John the Baptist appeared, preaching in the desert of Judea ²[and] saying, "Repent, for the kingdom of heaven is at hand!" ³It was of him that the prophet Isaiah had spoken when he said:

"A voice of one crying out in the desert,
'Prepare the way of the Lord,
    make straight his paths.'"

⁴John wore clothing made of camel's hair and had a leather belt around his waist. His food was locusts and wild honey. ⁵At that time Jerusalem, all Judea, and the whole region around the Jordan were going out to him ⁶and were being baptized by him in the Jordan River as they acknowledged their sins. . . .

¹³Then Jesus came from Galilee to John at the Jordan to be baptized by him. ¹⁴John tried to prevent him, saying, "I need to be baptized by you, and yet you are coming to me?" ¹⁵Jesus said to him in reply, "Allow it now, for thus it is fitting for us to fulfill all righteousness." Then he allowed him. ¹⁶After Jesus was baptized, he came up from the water and behold, the heavens were opened [for him], and he saw the Spirit of God descending like a dove [and] coming upon him. ¹⁷And a voice came from the heavens, saying, "This is my beloved Son, with whom I am well pleased."

John was certainly an imposing figure. By our sensibilities his garb of camel hair and leather and diet of locusts (bugs!) and wild honey mark him as a wild man, and he was no less so in his own time. His message, however, was not so much wild as radical—radical in the sense that it struck right to the center of Israel's identity without regard for the social standing of his audience. He is everything a biblical prophet is supposed to be. He proclaims a message from God, he speaks truth to power, and he gives notice of imminent judgment upon those who fail to heed his message: "Repent, for the kingdom of heaven is at hand!"

Matthew's gospel speaks of the kingdom of heaven in much the same way that Mark and Luke speak of the kingdom of God. Indeed, they are synonymous. Matthew probably prefers to call it the kingdom of heaven for traditional Jewish reasons, desiring to show respect for God's name by refraining from using it. For monotheists, "God" is certainly more than just a word or a title—it directly refers to the one, true Supreme Being, the creator of all.

Many in Israel clung to an idealized image of their past. Theirs was once a kingdom, a mighty power unbowed before its enemies, and assured of a perpetual royal lineage of noble kings descended from David and Solomon (see 2 Sam 7:16). In Jerusalem, its capital, was the temple that God himself had chosen to be his special home, his "footstool," on earth (see Ps 132:7). Indeed, God had chosen Israel, alone among all the nations of earth, to be his special people (2 Sam 7:23-24). That sense of security was in the distant past, however. During John the Baptist's life, King Herod and his descendants reigned only with Caesar's approval and they were in no way part of the Davidic lineage. Herod the Great had lavishly embellished the temple in Jerusalem, but the Sadducees who governed most of its operations were seen as being pro-Roman at the people's expense.

Many felt that God was withholding his glory from the temple and were awaiting a sudden return of the Lord there. This return was also associated with the appearance of a divine messenger, or the return of Elijah, the one whose role in divine prophecy Matthew associates with John the Baptist. "Now I am sending my messenger— / he will prepare the way before me; / And the lord whom you seek will come suddenly to his temple; / The messenger of the covenant whom you desire— / see, he is coming! says the LORD of hosts" (Mal 3:1).

Anyone hearing John announce that the kingdom of heaven was at hand might also have thought that John was the messenger proclaimed by Malachi. The anticipation of the arrival of God's kingdom must have been quite palpable among those who sought John's baptism. Many would have yearned for its appearance. God's rule meant a number of very important things. Israel's glory and independence would once again prevail in the world under a divinely anointed Davidic king. God would truly be present in the temple, shedding the light of his wisdom from Jerusalem to the far ends of the earth. But God's rule would also begin as a day of fierce judgment against Israel itself, which was why John's message came as a severe warning.

## Matthew 3:7-12

> [7]When he saw many of the Pharisees and Sadducees coming to his baptism, he said to them, "You brood of vipers! Who warned you to flee from the coming wrath? [8]Produce good fruit as evidence of your repentance. [9]And do not presume to say to yourselves, 'We have Abraham as our father.' For I tell you, God can raise up children to Abraham from these stones. [10]Even now the ax lies at the root of the trees. Therefore every tree that does not bear good fruit will be cut down and thrown into the fire. [11]I am baptizing you with water, for repentance, but the one who is coming after me is mightier than I. I am not worthy to carry his sandals. He will baptize you with the holy Spirit and fire. [12]His winnowing fan is in his hand. He will clear his threshing floor and gather his wheat into his barn, but the chaff he will burn with unquenchable fire."

John was certain that the kingdom of heaven was very near; it was "at hand," and he was also probably familiar with the prophecy of Amos (5:18-20) concerning its arrival:

> Woe to those who yearn
>   for the day of the LORD!
> What will the day of the LORD mean for you?
>   It will be darkness, not light!
> As if someone fled from a lion
>   and a bear met him;
> Or as if on entering the house
>   he rested his hand against the wall,
>   and a snake bit it.
> Truly, the day of the LORD will be darkness, not light,
>   gloom without any brightness!

John's call to baptism was a summons for all children of Israel to renew their relationship with God by entering the waters through which Israel first entered the Promised Land. They were to repent from all those sins and violations of the covenant for which "the day of the Lord" would come as a day of wrath.

John is God's messenger, but part of his message is that someone greater than he is coming, and when Jesus of Nazareth approaches him, seeking to be baptized by John, John hesitates. "I need to be baptized by you, and yet you are coming to me?" (Matt 3:14). Perhaps you sense John's problem. From what does Jesus need to repent? Let's examine how the four gospel writers handle this.

Many good biblical scholars have noted that Jesus receiving a baptism of repentance by John might cause embarrassment to Christians, who, from the very beginning, have believed firmly in Jesus' sinlessness (see Heb 4:15; 1 Pet 2:22; 1 John 3:5). Indeed, many good biblical scholars believe it is for this reason that the Gospel of John avoids mentioning that Jesus was baptized by John. Instead of describing Jesus' baptism, it tells of John simply seeing Jesus coming toward him when he proclaims, "Behold, the Lamb of God, who takes away the sin of the world" (John 1:29).

In Matthew, Jesus' response to John doesn't quite remove the puzzle. "Allow it now, for thus it is fitting for us to fulfill all righteousness." What does it mean to fulfill all righteousness? More than one meaning has been given over the ages. One of the more satisfying suggestions is that Jesus saw in John's baptism a divine call to bring to fulfillment that righteous purpose God had given to Jesus as his son. Some also see in Jesus' baptism a symbolic proclamation of the Gospel. Matthew has already portrayed Jesus as the ideal Israel when he associated Israel's exodus from Egypt with Jesus' own departure from Egypt as an infant (2:15). It could well be, then, that Matthew wants us to understand that Jesus sought John's baptism as an example to Israel, because God calls all Israel to fulfill their righteous obligations as God's firstborn (Exod 4:22). If we accept that Jesus submitted to baptism in order to lead others to do the same, then the assertion that Jesus' baptism sanctified the waters for our own baptism is more than just a pious notion.

In any event, Matthew says John needed convincing, and only because it fulfilled all righteousness did he allow Jesus to be baptized (3:14). When Jesus rose from the waters of the Jordan, John witnessed the heavens open and the Holy Spirit descend on Jesus "like a dove." This does not tell us the Spirit was shaped like a dove; it tells us that the

Holy Spirit alighted on Jesus calmly, as though finding a perch where it feels perfectly at home. Mark also says the Spirit descended like a dove, but only after "the heavens being torn open," and then, after the descent, the Spirit "drove" Jesus into the desert (Mark 1:10-12). Where Mark wants us to understand the urgency of Jesus' mission following his baptism, Matthew still wishes to emphasize Jesus' greater stature in comparison to John.

In Mark (and Luke), for example, it is Jesus who hears the voice from heaven proclaiming him as God's Son, in whom God is well pleased (Mark 1:11; Luke 3:22). That makes the proclamation a moment of deep intimacy between the Father and the Son. Matthew wants us to be sure that John heard the voice, though. Later on, John will still be asking for clarification for just who Jesus is (see Matt 11:2-6). But Matthew also wants us to hear the voice that is proclaimed not just to John, but to all: "This is my beloved Son, with whom I am well pleased." When we encounter Jesus in Scripture and sacrament, we let the words echo in our hearts.

## THE SECOND MYSTERY OF LIGHT

### The Wedding at Cana

*John 2:1-12*

> [1]On the third day there was a wedding in Cana in Galilee, and the mother of Jesus was there. [2]Jesus and his disciples were also invited to the wedding. [3]When the wine ran short, the mother of Jesus said to him, "They have no wine." [4][And] Jesus said to her, "Woman, how does your concern affect me? My hour has not yet come." [5]His mother said to the servers, "Do whatever he tells you." [6]Now there were six stone water jars there for Jewish ceremonial washings, each holding twenty to thirty gallons. [7]Jesus told them, "Fill the jars with water." So they filled them to the brim. [8]Then he told them, "Draw some out now and take it to the headwaiter." So they took it. [9]And when the headwaiter tasted the water that had become wine, without knowing where it came from (although the servers who had drawn the water knew), the headwaiter called the bridegroom [10]and said to him, "Everyone serves good wine first, and then when people have drunk freely, an inferior one; but you have kept the good wine until now." [11]Jesus did this as the beginning of his signs in Cana in Galilee and so revealed his glory, and his disciples began to believe in him.

[12]After this, he and his mother, [his] brothers, and his disciples
went down to Capernaum and stayed there only a few days.

Jesus and his disciples are guests at a wedding in Cana, the hosts run
out of wine, and Mary informs Jesus of the situation. His response to her
seems curt to our ears. After all, who calls his mother "woman"? The
questions start to mount. Why are Jesus and his disciples at a wedding?
Elsewhere, doesn't Jesus see weddings as out of keeping with preparation for the kingdom (see Matt 24:37-39; Luke 17:26-27)? Is Mary actually
asking Jesus to do something about it? What would she expect him to
do? We know of no reason why Mary would ask him to do something
miraculous—this, after all, will be Jesus' first sign. What does that mean?
And his response to his mother implies that he feels she is pushing him
into entering his "hour." What is Jesus' hour?

Exploring some of the elements behind these questions will reveal
what makes this a sign. In our day, we most often think of signs as
important alerts or directional information on a roadway, that is, when
they aren't just advertising something for us to buy. Any questions we
seek to answer about this first sign in John should alert us to the depth of
meaning in a sign from Jesus. As we investigate the sign, we will see that
John's brief description of the wedding in Cana is packed with biblical
allusions to prophetic promises of God's salvation.

Jesus' signs are not simply miracles; they are a revelation of the eternal
life that is to be found in Jesus alone. Miracles might amaze even skeptics,
but a sign is meant to lead anyone who witnesses it into deeper contemplation. A sign points to something beyond itself, something bigger and
more important than itself, however amazing the sign itself might seem.

Part of the significance of this sign is that it happens at a wedding.
Elsewhere in the gospels, Jesus suggests that the cultural attention given
to weddings can be a grave distraction from seeing the signs of God's
ultimate activity in the world: "As it was in the days of Noah, so it will be
in the days of the Son of Man; they were eating and drinking, marrying
and giving in marriage up to the day that Noah entered the ark, and the
flood came and destroyed them all" (Luke 17:26-27; see Matt 24:37-39).
Here in John, the giving in marriage with its indulgence in festive eating
and drinking is actually a vital part of Jesus' sign.

In the Bible, marriage is vital to the entire human project. Marriages
bring about offspring, and children are the visible sign of hope for a
future beyond one's self. Marriage means one's family will go on and

one's name will be remembered, and hopefully blessed by succeeding generations. Just look at the importance of genealogies in the biblical record: 1 Chronicles 1–8; Matthew 1:1-17; Luke 3:23-38. But marriages were also a way of obtaining and sealing power.

Kings David and Solomon were only two of Judah's kings to enter in multiple marriages to secure political alliances with neighboring kingdoms. When God sent Jeremiah to warn Judah that its idolatry and injustice were leading it to destruction, he forbade Jeremiah to marry or to have children because of Judah's impending doom (Jer 16:2). Jesus' own celibacy is chiefly regarded as a sign that the messianic age was at hand, and Paul urged those who could to embrace celibacy in order to focus on serving the Lord, whose return he believed to be imminent (1 Cor 7:29-32).

In the Synoptic Gospels Jesus also clearly teaches that marriage will not be part of resurrected life: "When they rise from the dead, they neither marry nor are given in marriage, but they are like the angels in heaven" (Mark 12:25). There is one marriage, however, that is the ultimate symbol of what Jesus' mission was all about. The Old Testament prophets made it clearly known that when God fulfilled his promises to Israel, a fulfillment that was expected to be brought about by the Messiah, it would be a very special marriage, a marriage between God and his bride:

> For as a young man marries a virgin,
>> your Builder shall marry you;
> And as a bridegroom rejoices in his bride
>> so shall your God rejoice in you. (Isa 62:5)

Weddings were then, as now, times for feasting, and in addition to the symbol of a wedding, a frequent symbol of the messianic era was a magnificent feast:

> On this mountain the LORD of hosts
>> will provide for all peoples
> A feast of rich food and choice wines,
>> juicy, rich food and pure, choice wines. (Isa 25:6)

In John, Jesus begins his ministry at a wedding and his only involvement in the wedding that we are told of is that he is the one who ultimately provides the choice wine. In doing so, Jesus is not just participating in a particular wedding on a particular day in Cana. He is making this wedding a sign to his disciples that in him the glory of the ultimate wedding between God and his people has begun to take place.

Why, then, did Jesus react as he did when his mother told him, "They have no wine" (2:3)? First, he calls his mother "woman," and then he tells her, "how does your concern affect me? My hour has not yet come." The late Raymond Brown, one of the foremost scholars of John's gospel in modern times, suggests that Jesus spoke to his mother as "woman" in part because she will be the woman who will be with him when his hour does come. Jesus' hour, in John, is the time of his passion, death, and resurrection. They are the events that mark the ultimate "hour" in which Jesus is fully glorified. From the cross, Jesus will speak to his mother once again, and he will place her in a special relationship to the unnamed disciple "whom he loved":

> When Jesus saw his mother and the disciple there whom he loved, he said to his mother, "Woman, behold, your son." Then he said to the disciple, "Behold, your mother." And from that hour the disciple took her into his home. (John 19:26-27)

When Jesus calls his mother "woman," rather than being insulting, it marks her full relationship to him as one more important to Jesus than their biological relationship alone. Mary is more than his mother—she is to be *the* new mother, the Eve of a new creation, a new family of humanity, the mother of all his disciples.

In telling her son that the wedding hosts were out of wine, Mary was seemingly asking Jesus to be responsive to a mundane affair, one that was not his responsibility. Jesus, however, knew that if he acted he would be setting in place the events that would inextricably lead to the "hour" of his glory on the cross and in the resurrection. No other gospel goes to the extent that John does in portraying Jesus' crucifixion and resurrection as a single event, the hour of Jesus' glorification. In John, immediately after Judas leaves the scene of the Last Supper to betray Jesus, Jesus says, "Now is the Son of Man glorified, and God is glorified in him" (John 13:31). His death is an intimate part of his hour of glory, because, as he told the crowd in John 12:32, "when I am lifted up from the earth, I will draw everyone to myself."

It is a peculiar feature of John's gospel that there is no description of the institution of the Eucharist during the Last Supper. Instead, John alone describes the washing of the disciples' feet at that time, followed by the announcement of his impending betrayal (13:1-30). No other gospel, however, devotes so much space to proclaiming the reality of Jesus' presence in the eucharistic elements. This is chiefly done in the bread of life discourse (6:22-59), but many scholars are convinced that Jesus' transformation of water to wine at the wedding in Cana would immediately remind John's community of the unique transformation of wine that manifests Christ's true presence in their celebration of Eucharist.

Jesus' glory is made manifest to his disciples at the wedding in Cana. Christians who desire to heighten their own awareness of his glory might begin by taking to mind Mary's trust in her Son when she told the servers, "Do whatever he tells you" (2:5).

## THE THIRD MYSTERY OF LIGHT
### The Proclamation of the Kingdom of God
*Mark 1:14-15*

> [14]After John had been arrested, Jesus came to Galilee proclaiming the gospel of God: [15]"This is the time of fulfillment. The kingdom of God is at hand. Repent, and believe in the gospel."

Jesus' ministry begins in earnest when John the Baptist's ends. On one level, their core messages seem to have shared a very special interest: the kingdom of God, what in the Gospel of Matthew is usually called "the kingdom of heaven."

> In those days John the Baptist appeared, preaching in the desert of Judea [and] saying, "Repent, for the kingdom of heaven is at hand!" (Matt 3:1-2)

As was mentioned earlier concerning the Lord's baptism, Matthew, the most Jewish of all the gospels, is thought to have substituted "heaven" for "God" because pious Jews of his time refrained from frequent use of God's name out of respect for the commandment, "You shall not invoke the name of the LORD, your God, in vain. For the LORD will not leave unpunished anyone who invokes his name in vain" (Exod 20:7). We also looked at why the kingdom of God was so important to John's call to baptize for the repentance of sin. John was certain that the arrival of God's kingdom would be a day of severe judgment.

"Even now the ax lies at the root of the trees. Therefore every tree that does not bear good fruit will be cut down and thrown into the fire. I am baptizing you with water, for repentance, but the one who is coming after me is mightier than I. I am not worthy to carry his sandals. He will baptize you with the holy Spirit and fire. His winnowing fan is in his hand. He will clear his threshing floor and gather his wheat into his barn, but the chaff he will burn with unquenchable fire." (Matt 3:10-12)

Jesus also proclaims the nearness of God's kingdom and he also calls everyone to repentance. But there is a big difference between the way Jesus' ministry revealed the nearness of the kingdom and the impending doom John associated with it. Jesus also warned of a coming day of judgment (see Matt 24:15-31), but the primary focus of his ministry was to announce a time of God's favor, as when he quoted the prophet Isaiah in his hometown synagogue (Luke 4:18-19):

"The Spirit of the Lord is upon me,
   because he has anointed me
      to bring glad tidings to the poor.
He sent me to proclaim liberty to captives
   and recovery of sight to the blind,
      to let the oppressed go free,
and to proclaim a year acceptable to the Lord."

The stark difference in emphasis between John's dire warnings concerning the nearness of the kingdom and Jesus' message of glad tidings to the poor, liberty for captives, and healing for the disabled left John with a question about Jesus:

When John heard in prison of the works of the Messiah, he sent his disciples to him with this question, "Are you the one who is to come, or should we look for another?" Jesus said to them in reply, "Go and tell John what you hear and see: the blind regain their sight, the lame walk, lepers are cleansed, the deaf hear, the dead are raised, and the poor have the good news proclaimed to them. And blessed is the one who takes no offense at me." (Matt 11:2-6)

When Jesus proclaimed the nearness of the kingdom of God, he not only spoke about it, but he demonstrated what it meant to live in the realm where God's authority prevailed. God's kingdom is an unimaginable treasure, one worth sacrificing everything else in life in order to enter that kingdom:

"The kingdom of heaven is like a treasure buried in a field, which a person finds and hides again, and out of joy goes and sells all that he has and buys that field. Again, the kingdom of heaven is like a merchant searching for fine pearls. When he finds a pearl of great price, he goes and sells all that he has and buys it." (Matt 13:44-46)

Those who listened carefully to Jesus' parables of the kingdom would not fail to hear in them a call to conversion and the need for repentance. Selling all that one has in order to obtain the kingdom warns that the more one clings to the goods of an earthly kingdom, the less likely one will obtain the unequaled treasure of the kingdom of heaven. Not everyone who hears the Good News of the kingdom of heaven will be able to enter it:

"Again, the kingdom of heaven is like a net thrown into the sea, which collects fish of every kind. When it is full they haul it ashore and sit down to put what is good into buckets. What is bad they throw away." (Matt 13:47-48)

Indeed, not everyone who heard the Good News was capable of responding to it with complete abandon. Even though they recognized its promise, their cares, concerns, and possessions could still come between them and the kingdom of heaven.

When he spoke about the kingdom, Jesus usually did so in the context of a short story, called a parable. His parables had a great depth of meaning that went far beyond just the simple details of the stories. Each of his parables tugged at the imagination because the outcome of the story would often defy common sense. In order to make sense of his parables, those who heard them would have to accept that the way God acted in his kingdom was not the way people usually expected things to go. In the parable of the Sower and the Seed and his explanation of it (Matt 13:3-8, 18-23), Jesus likens his preaching of the kingdom to a farmer who scatters his seeds freely, liberally, without regard for the quality of soil upon which it landed. This is not what farmers did in Jesus' day. Seed was valuable, only so much would have been saved after a harvest for replanting, and they knew where to plant to maximize their yield.

What could this extravagant, even foolish-seeming, sowing of valuable seed be saying about the kingdom of heaven? The Good News of the kingdom is freely proclaimed to all, whether or not they are truly prepared to respond to it, but not everyone takes it to heart. The Good News, though proclaimed to all, is also proclaimed in a somewhat hidden, mysterious manner. Jesus' parables are like seeds: only those who are prepared to ponder their meaning, like good soil holds onto and nurtures a seed, will discover their full meaning, when the seed sprouts, takes root, and produces its substantial yield.

When questioned by his disciples as to why Jesus taught in parables, Jesus' answer often proves puzzling, as in this passage:

> The disciples approached him and said, "Why do you speak to them in parables?" He said to them in reply, "Because knowledge of the mysteries of the kingdom of heaven has been granted to you, but to them it has not been granted. To anyone who has, more will be given and he will grow rich; from anyone who has not, even what he has will be taken away. This is why I speak to them in parables, because 'they look but do not see and hear but do not listen or understand.'" (Matt 13:10-13)

His answer suggests that Jesus was acutely aware of his parables' powers to arouse curiosity in those who genuinely possessed a spiritual hunger. The hungry would ponder and parse his parables and those who yearned to hear the goodness in his Good News would find it and, finding it, come back to him for more. They are the ones who have and to whom more would be given.

Jesus is not pessimistic about the power of his message to attract followers, however. He expects the message of the kingdom to eventually have tremendous success. It has growing power like a mustard seed:

> He proposed another parable to them. "The kingdom of heaven is like a mustard seed that a person took and sowed in a field. It is the smallest of all the seeds, yet when full-grown it is the largest of plants. It becomes a large bush, and the 'birds of the sky come and dwell in its branches.'" (Matt 13:31-32)

And the transforming growth of yeast in dough:

> He spoke to them another parable. "The kingdom of heaven is like yeast that a woman took and mixed with three measures of wheat flour until the whole batch was leavened." (Matt 13:33)

In every miracle Jesus performed, at the heart of all his teaching, in the examples that he set and in the mission that he entrusted to his disciples (to which all Christians are entrusted by their baptism into Christ), Jesus sought to make the kingdom of God a present reality. The fullness of the kingdom is yet to come, but its entrance in this world became a reality with Jesus' ministry and he commissioned his followers also to be a sign of its reality:

> Then he summoned his twelve disciples and gave them authority over unclean spirits to drive them out and to cure every disease and every illness. (Matt 10:1)

Jesus brought the Good News of the kingdom to the poor, the downtrodden, the sick, and the disabled, but he also brought it to sinners. At the very heart of the Good News of the kingdom of God is the promise of God's mercy and forgiveness to any who seek it through repentance. Jesus proclaimed a profound extravagance of mercy in God's kingdom. Perhaps no parable better illustrates this than the parable popularly known as the Prodigal Son (Luke 15:11-32). The joy of the prodigal's father in welcoming his wayward son back into family life reflects the joy in heaven when any one of us turns away from sin to welcome life in the kingdom of God:

> [T]here will be more joy in heaven over one sinner who repents than over ninety-nine righteous people who have no need of repentance. (Luke 15:7)

*Feb 8*

## THE FOURTH MYSTERY OF LIGHT

### The Transfiguration

*Luke 9:28-36*

> [28]About eight days after he said this, he took Peter, John, and James and went up the mountain to pray. [29]While he was praying his face changed in appearance and his clothing became dazzling white. [30]And behold, two men were conversing with him, Moses and Elijah, [31]who appeared in glory and spoke of his exodus that he was going to accomplish in Jerusalem. [32]Peter and his companions had been overcome by sleep, but becoming fully awake, they saw his glory and the two men standing with him. [33]As they were about to part from him, Peter said to Jesus, "Master, it is good that we are here; let us make three tents, one for you, one for Moses, and one for Elijah." But he did not know what he was saying. [34]While he was still speaking, a cloud came and cast a shadow over them, and they became frightened when they entered the cloud. [35]Then from the cloud came a voice that said, "This is my chosen Son; listen to him."

³⁶After the voice had spoken, Jesus was found alone. They fell silent and did not at that time tell anyone what they had seen.

The account of Jesus' transfiguration appears in each of the Synoptic Gospels (Matt 17:1-9; Mark 9:2-11; Luke 9:28-36). In reflecting on Luke's account in particular, it is worth noting that there are two pertinent themes there. One of them is stressed in his account of the transfiguration, but absent in Matthew and Mark's accounts. In Luke, we most often find Jesus either dining with others (there are ten meals with Jesus depicted in Luke) or deeply engaged in prayer. Only Luke specifically mentions that the transfiguration takes place when Jesus goes up a mountain to pray. That Jesus ascends a mountain to pray is probably meant to alert us to Jesus' desire for an especially intimate exchange with his Father. Mountaintops in Scripture are often places where divine appearances (theophanies) occur, as when God appeared to Moses on the mountain called both Horeb and Sinai (Exod 19:16-25), or when God spoke to Elijah from the same mountain (1 Kgs 19:3-13).

When Moses spoke with the Lord on Mount Sinai, his face became so radiant that he had to wear a veil when later speaking to the Israelites (Exod 34:29-35). The mountain that tradition associates with the transfiguration is Mount Tabor, located between Nazareth and the southwestern shore of the Sea of Galilee. Jesus takes Peter, James, and John (the Zebedee brothers) with him. These three disciples, along with Andrew, appear to be especially close to Jesus, for they are the disciples most frequently mentioned by name in the gospels. As close as they are to Jesus, they are "overcome" by sleep while Jesus prays. Perhaps Luke tells us this so that we will not be surprised that all his remaining disciples (the eleven that remain after Judas's departure) will sleep when Jesus prays at the Mount of Olives immediately before his arrest, trial, and crucifixion (Luke 22:39-46).

Jesus, deep in prayer, is transfigured—his face is changed in an un-described manner and his clothing becomes "dazzling white." Mark emphasizes that no earthly launderer could ever have made his clothing look so brilliant (Mark 9:3). The emphasis on his clothing is greater than that concerning his face, but there is a reason for that. In New Testament times the clothing people wore designated their status in relation to the rest of society. The greater one's status, the more distinctive one's clothing. Jesus' clothing is dazzling beyond compare and this is just one sign given during the transfiguration of his divine dignity. While the three disciples are sleeping, two of the greatest prophets of Israel, both of whom received special revelations from God, appear to Jesus and engage in conversation with him. Moses and Elijah's appearances were also bathed in glory. Up until this point, nothing has been noted by Luke to distinguish between their glory and Jesus' glory. This appears to be deliberate, a skillful literary tactic that will add emphasis to what follows.

When Peter, James, and John awake, they witness the incredible scene, but up until this point, the event itself has been described as a private one between Jesus, Moses, and Elijah. Only Luke records the private conversation, through which Jesus' disciples had slept. The topic of discussion will inextricably link the purpose of Jesus' mission with God's purpose in calling Moses and Elijah to be his prophets in the Old Testament era. It is the exodus that Jesus will accomplish in Jerusalem that engages Moses and Elijah's interest in Jesus. The exodus associated with Moses brought about the birth of God's covenant people, Israel, and the preservation of that covenant was the focus of Elijah's prophetic ministry.

In mentioning the exodus in association with Jesus, Luke swiftly and deftly unites the purpose of Jesus' forthcoming death with the original exodus, uniting the whole of salvation history within a single theme. Throughout history and culminating in the death and resurrection of Christ, God's saving deeds have had a single intention, to create for God a people who, through a timeless covenant, will be free to worship God in freedom and righteousness. Luke has been very consistent in proclaiming this theme. It is at the heart of the *Benedictus*, the canticle Zechariah exclaimed at the birth of his son, John the Baptist:

> Blessed be the Lord, the God of Israel,
>> for he has visited and brought redemption to his people.
> He has raised up a horn for our salvation
>> within the house of David his servant,
> even as he promised through the mouth of his holy prophets from
>> of old:
>> salvation from our enemies and from the hand of all who hate us,
> to show mercy to our fathers
>> and to be mindful of his holy covenant
> and of the oath he swore to Abraham our father,
>> and to grant us that,
> rescued from the hand of enemies,
>> without fear we might worship him in holiness and righteousness
>> before him all our days. (Luke 1:68-75)

Moses and Elijah appeared with Jesus in glory, according to Luke 9:31, but in contrast to Mark, Luke is careful not to emphasize their glory in relation to Jesus. When Peter, James, and John awake, they see Jesus' glory, but Moses and Elijah are simply "the two men standing with him" (9:32). In this way Luke prepares us to recognize the mistake Peter is about to make. After recognizing who the two men are, and ever the one to speak rashly without understanding (see Luke 9:19-22; 22:33-34), Peter exclaims to Jesus, "[L]et us make three tents, one for you, one for Moses, and one for Elijah" (9:33). Peter "did not know what he was saying." There is to be no comparison of Moses and Elijah's dignity with that of Jesus. While God did speak directly to Moses from a cloud on Sinai (Exod 19:9) and to Elijah through "a light silent sound" (1 Kgs 19:12), the voice that speaks through a cloud during Jesus' transfiguration makes it very clear who brings us the ultimate revelation of God: "This is my chosen Son; listen to him" (9:35).

Without mentioning the departure of the cloud after the voice has spoken, we are told "Jesus was found alone" (9:36). It is intended to be understood as a revelation. It is Jesus alone who will bring about the fulfillment of salvation history. Moses and Elijah are only prefaces to this greater story.

Why did the three disciples with Jesus at his transfiguration fall silent? Why wouldn't they immediately tell the other disciples what they had seen with their own eyes? Perhaps it was too momentous a thing to speak about. Perhaps, as they descended the mountain, they were too occupied with trying to take it all in. The event they had just witnessed was unquestionably about Jesus' identity as God's beloved Son, but the disciples had a lot to juggle in their minds concerning the fullness of Jesus' identity. Luke tells us that just days before they had gone up the mountain, Jesus asked his disciples some very important questions about his identity, but when Peter answered, he was rebuked, they were all told to keep quiet, and then Jesus told them something horrible.

> Once when Jesus was praying in solitude, and the disciples were with him, he asked them, "Who do the crowds say that I am?" They said in reply, "John the Baptist; others, Elijah; still others, 'One of the ancient prophets has arisen.'" Then he said to them, "But who do you say that I am?" Peter said in reply, "The Messiah of God." He rebuked them and directed them not to tell this to anyone.
>
> He said, "The Son of Man must suffer greatly and be rejected by the elders, the chief priests, and the scribes, and be killed and on the third day be raised." (Luke 9:18-22)

Scripture and tradition (especially as found in early ecumenical councils) teach us very clearly who Jesus is, but his disciples only learned slowly, through their experiences with him. Nothing they saw, heard, or experienced was enough to keep them from abandoning him when the time came for his arrest and crucifixion. It would take something more than the transfiguration to convince them what the titles "Son of God" and "Messiah" truly meant. Conversely, it may be that many Christians today feel certain of their faith in Jesus Christ as true God and true man, but our faith will also have to grow through our experiences. Immediately after warning his disciples of his own destiny of suffering and rejection, he told them, "If anyone wishes to come after me, he must deny himself and take up his cross daily and follow me" (Luke 9:23).

## THE FIFTH MYSTERY OF LIGHT

### The Institution of the Eucharist

*1 Corinthians 11:23-26*

> [23]For I received from the Lord what I also handed on to you, that the Lord Jesus, on the night he was handed over, took bread, [24]and, after he had given thanks, broke it and said, "This is my body that is for you. Do this in remembrance of me." [25]In the same way also the cup, after supper, saying, "This cup is the new covenant in my blood. Do this, as often as you drink it, in remembrance of me." [26]For as often as you eat this bread and drink the cup, you proclaim the death of the Lord until he comes.

The apostle Paul forever impressed his stamp on Christianity. His numerous letters fill most of the New Testament following the four gospels and Acts (where he is a major figure). Paul's message of salvation in Christ was firmly anchored in his experience of meeting the risen Christ while on his way to persecute the early believers in Christ in Damascus.

It took a while for him to sort out that experience. After he was baptized he went into the desert of Arabia to contemplate what it all meant and what he was to do with his life now that he had been so clearly called by Christ (Gal 1:15-18). Paul came to realize that the essence of the Good News lay in preaching Jesus as the Messiah (the Christ) whose death on a cross meant the forgiveness of sins and whose resurrection from the dead meant eternal life. In his own words, Paul tells the Corinthians, "I resolved to know nothing while I was with you except Jesus Christ, and him crucified" (1 Cor 2:2). This was the Good News for Jew or Gentile, for anyone who embraced Christ by faith.

Unlike the four gospels, each of which recounts many of Jesus' teachings, acts of healing, and his relationship to his followers, especially the twelve whom he named apostles, Paul wrote very little about all that Jesus said and did before his death and resurrection. Perhaps Paul knew he could not compete with the apostles who had followed Christ during his ministry when it came to recounting Jesus' teaching and ministry. Paul could, however, claim equal stature to them as a witness to the resurrection of the crucified Christ (see 1 Cor 9:1). And Paul quickly realized that it was the message of a crucified and resurrected Savior that electrified—converted!—so many Gentiles. Paul had his own way of teaching the importance of virtuous living. He urged his followers to live according to the Spirit given to them by Christ (Rom 8:3-4).

This makes it all the more interesting when Paul reminds the Corinthians of the important role that the Last Supper is meant to play in their worship: "For I received from the Lord what I also handed on to you" (1 Cor 11:23). Paul was not at the Last Supper, but he insisted on its importance to Christian worship. Paul's account strongly resembles the Last Supper accounts of the Synoptic Gospels and Luke's in particular. Paul did not learn about the Last Supper from any of the four gospels, however. Indeed, Paul's account of the Last Supper is the very first written record we have of the Last Supper. Paul wrote First Corinthians around AD 56, but Luke's gospel wasn't written until sometime between AD 80 and 90.

That Paul wrote of the Last Supper as a liturgical practice he had received "from the Lord" and had previously handed on to the Corinthians tells us three very important things. First, the Lord's Supper (what we refer to as the Eucharist) was an essential part of Christian worship from the beginning of the faith. Paul's early account of the Last Supper bears striking similarities to the much later accounts found in the gospels. This tells us that the tradition of celebrating Eucharist as the Lord's Supper (the Last Supper) was handed on consistently and accurately throughout the early church.

Second, when Paul says he received the tradition of celebrating the Lord's Supper "from the Lord," he doesn't mean the risen Lord told him how to celebrate the Last Supper. It means the tradition of celebrating the Lord's Supper that Paul received was an authentic one, one that came down to him with the authority of those who had been participants when Christ instituted the Eucharist at the Last Supper, and so Paul had indeed received it from the Lord, because that is from whom the early apostles had received it.

Finally, we discover in the importance Paul placed on handing on this essential tradition the importance of what is often called "big T Tradition" to Christian faith. The essence of who we are, what we believe, and how we worship are to be handed on, and they are handed on to us by the church with divine authority.

## Luke 22:15-16

> [15] He said to them, "I have eagerly desired to eat this Passover with you before I suffer, [16] for, I tell you, I shall not eat it [again] until there is fulfillment in the kingdom of God."

We all eat to stay alive. Many in the world do not eat enough, including millions of children. Others, children and adults alike, eat far too much of the wrong foods, and so risk their health and shorten their lives. The truth remains, however, that we all eat to stay alive. In biblical times Israelites ate their food with a profound recognition that the bounty of the earth was a life-sustaining gift from their God, the Creator of all:

> The eyes of all look hopefully to you;
>     you give them their food in due season.
> You open wide your hand
>     and satisfy the desire of every living thing. (Ps 145:15-16)

Eating, then as now, often brought together family and friends, but shared meals in biblical times were more likely to be regarded as religious events by all who dined together. Sharing a meal together was sharing life together, and life was sincerely regarded as a gift of God, never to be taken for granted. The Creator gives life, the Creator sustains life, and the Creator joins our lives together in life-giving relationships. The relationship enjoined by sharing a meal in biblical times was known as a covenant of salt—salt being the spice that both preserves food and makes it palatable.

Jesus' time was a time of religious turmoil, with the pagan Romans in strict control of Israel. The most devout people were divided between various religious sects, each of which regarded members of opposing sects as sinners and all of them certain that the common people of the land, the *anawim*, were hopeless sinners. Anyone intent on living in accord with God's commandments would have been careful not to join in a covenant of salt with sinners. Sharing God's gift of life with sinners would do more than ruin one's reputation; for a religious figure to do so it might even be considered blasphemous. Jesus ate with sinners, even with the worst sorts of sinners:

> The tax collectors and sinners were all drawing near to listen to him, but the Pharisees and scribes began to complain, saying, "This man welcomes sinners and eats with them." (Luke 15:1-2)

> A Pharisee invited him to dine with him, and he entered the Pharisee's house and reclined at table. Now there was a sinful woman in the city who learned that he was at table in the house of the Pharisee. Bringing an alabaster flask of ointment, she stood behind him at his feet weeping and began to bathe his feet with her tears. Then she wiped them with her hair, kissed them, and anointed them with the ointment. When the Pharisee who had invited him saw this he said to himself, "If this man were a prophet, he would know who and what sort of woman this is who is touching him, that she is a sinner." (Luke 7:36-39)

Robert Karris, a noted Franciscan biblical scholar, has gone so far as to assert that Jesus was killed because of the way he ate—because he ate with sinners. Jesus' meals with sinners probably wouldn't have endangered his life if he hadn't strongly suggested that there was a very special religious significance to meals in his presence. He likened his meals with others as a wedding feast, a meal with the bridegroom. The bride was Israel and God was welcoming all, including sinners, to the meal that was to inaugurate the kingdom of God (Matt 22:2; Luke 5:30-34; 14:15-24).

In Luke, Jesus is often depicted as either going to a meal or coming from a meal throughout the gospel. The ultimate meal with Jesus is, of course, the Last Supper. The Last Supper was Jesus' celebration of the Passover with his closest followers, including Judas, who would choose the occasion to betray him. The Passover meal is to this day the Jewish feast celebrating their freedom to both worship God and identify themselves as God's covenant people. It is a memorial feast that makes them participants in the exodus, God's great work of salvation in liberating them from slavery in Egypt.

At the Last Supper, Jesus celebrates this Jewish feast as a Jew with his Jewish disciples, but he interprets the feast in such a way that his disciples will forevermore celebrate it, not as the Jewish Passover, or even Jesus' last meal, but as *the* meal that brings their lives into communion with his life. After the resurrection they will call it "the Lord's Supper," and, far from being just an annual feast, they will celebrate it frequently, at least every Sunday, the day on which he rose from the dead. Whenever they "break bread," together they will remember how he broke the bread and blessed the cup, saying, "This is my body, which will be given for you; do this in memory of me," and "This cup is the new covenant in my blood, which will be shed for you" (Luke 22:19-20).

When we gather for Mass, when we celebrate Eucharist, we are celebrating our citizenship in the kingdom of God, which yet awaits fulfillment but is fully present in Christ who is truly present in the elements of the sacrament—in the proclaiming of the Word, in the person of the celebrant, and in the fellowship of all those assembled.

End

# CHAPTER 3

# The Sorrowful Mysteries

## THE FIRST SORROWFUL MYSTERY

### The Agony in the Garden

*Luke 22:39-46*

> [39]Then going out he went, as was his custom, to the Mount of Olives, and the disciples followed him. [40]When he arrived at the place he said to them, "Pray that you may not undergo the test." [41]After withdrawing about a stone's throw from them and kneeling, he prayed, [42]saying, "Father, if you are willing, take this cup away from me; still, not my will but yours be done." [[43]And to strengthen him an angel from heaven appeared to him. [44]He was in such agony and he prayed so fervently that his sweat became like drops of blood falling on the ground.] [45]When he rose from prayer and returned to his disciples, he found them sleeping from grief. [46]He said to them, "Why are you sleeping? Get up and pray that you may not undergo the test."

The name of this mystery reveals the age-old habit of Christians to blend the gospel accounts together. Just as we learn early on to retell the story of Jesus' birth by mixing Matthew's account with Luke's as best we can, so it is that in retelling Jesus' passion we often gather bits from all four gospels to compile what we hope is the most complete account as possible. There is some value in this, in that all the accounts have much to offer for prayer and contemplation. If we never carefully examine any one account on its own terms, however, we miss the special perspective a particular gospel wishes to give us.

Only Luke tells us that Jesus experienced agony in his prayer, but Luke never mentions that it took place in a garden. He simply refers to it as "the Mount of Olives." Scholars are pretty sure that Luke was very familiar with Mark's gospel, and Mark (and Matthew, following Mark) places Jesus' prayer in the Garden of Gethsemane. Tradition locates the Garden of Gethsemane at the foot of the Mount of Olives, so there is probably no contradiction between Mark and Luke, but the difference between Mark and Luke is still important.

Luke has previously informed his readers that Jesus has been in Jerusalem for a while, teaching in the temple by day, but spending his evenings "at the place called the Mount of Olives." On this night of nights he returns with his disciples to the mount "as was his custom" (Luke 22:39). Luke has his own customs, and one in particular is to tell us that when Jesus wants to spend time in prayer, he does so on a mountain, because that is where encounters with God customarily happen (see Luke 6:12; 9:28-36).

Having just shared his last meal with his disciples and knowing that Judas is busily engaged in his betrayal, Jesus' thoughts turn first toward his disciples, whom he urges to pray not to undergo the test. This is not any test they are to ask to be delivered from, but *the* test. This is the test Jesus himself is just entering: the *final* test. They should know how to pray for this, for he has taught them how:

> He was praying in a certain place, and when he had finished, one of his disciples said to him, "Lord, teach us to pray just as John taught his disciples." He said to them, "When you pray, say:
>
>> Father, hallowed be your name,
>>     your kingdom come.
>>     Give us each day our daily bread
>>     and forgive us our sins
>>     for we ourselves forgive everyone in debt to us,
>>     and do not subject us to the final test." (Luke 11:1-4)

Prior to the scene at the Mount of Olives, the most famous test in Sacred Scripture was the test God put to Abraham when he asked him to sacrifice his son Isaac. A biblical synonym for "test" is "temptation." When a righteous person is put to a test, the test is a temptation to cease being good in order to escape an evil experience. In Luke, after Jesus' baptism, the devil tempted Jesus in the wilderness. Jesus was victorious in that round of testing by ultimately rebuking the devil with the words, "You shall not put the Lord, your God, to the test." But the devil had not finished with putting Jesus to the test. Luke says, "When the devil had finished every temptation, he departed from him for a time" (4:12-13).

The final test, or temptation, is all or nothing. To pass the final test one must be willing to endure persecution and even a brutal death. On the Mount of Olives, Jesus experiences the devil's final temptation. After urging his disciples to pray for themselves, Jesus withdrew from his disciples "about a stone's throw from them." Kneeling in prayer, Jesus asks if (and only if) it is his Father's will that "this cup" will be taken away from him. A cup, which might hold a very heady drink, is spoken of in Scripture as an event of great turmoil that God has prepared for someone or some people or nations to drink. The prophets Isaiah, Jeremiah, and Habakkuk all speak of a cup of God's wrath (Isa 51:17, 22; Jer 25:15; Hab 2:15).

In Matthew and Mark Jesus speaks of the "cup" he will have to drink (Matt 20:22-23; Mark 10:38-39) in chastising James and John for seeking power (either through their mother in Matthew or on their own behalf in Mark) when Jesus came to rule in his kingdom. Jesus chastises them by warning that the kingdom they wish to rule in will come only after Jesus drinks the cup that he must drink. It is a reference to his death by crucifixion. Luke makes no reference to Jesus' employing the symbol of a cup before this prayer on the Mount of Olives, except in one very important place. Luke does record Jesus associating a cup with his death at the Last Supper. There Jesus takes the cup after they had eaten and says, "This cup is the new covenant in my blood, which will be shed for you" (Luke 22:20).

Now, in prayer to his Father, Jesus prays that he may not have to drink the cup filled with suffering after all—but only if God wills to take it from him. You will notice that verses 43 and 44, the verses that speak of the angel coming to strengthen him and the greatness of his agony, are in brackets. They do not appear in some of the most ancient texts we have of Luke, but that doesn't mean they were added to Luke's account. There is reason to believe that some scribes may have deliberately deleted them in copying Luke's text, because they made Jesus seem too human in an age when certain theologians were claiming that Jesus lacked true divinity. In any event, they are canonical and are inspired Scripture.

The challenge for today's Christians is to embrace Jesus as both fully human and fully divine, with his divinity never cancelling out his human frailty. As we read in the New Testament letter to the Hebrews (4:15-16), we can confidently approach the throne of grace to receive mercy because "we do not have a high priest who is unable to sympathize with our weaknesses, but one who has similarly been tested in every way, yet without sin."

There is, however, a great strength in Jesus' agony. The Greek word for our English "agony" is *agonia*, and it has a rich association in Greek literature with the courageous fortitude shown by athletes. There, agony is not just pain, but it is the struggle to bring all one's strength to a physical endeavor in which one wishes to triumph. In mentioning Jesus' agony in prayer, Luke is telling us that Jesus is pitting himself against the temptation to push his cup, his forthcoming crucifixion, aside, and he succeeds, because of the effort he puts into prayer.

Luke emphasizes the courageous vigor with which Jesus enters his duel with temptation by use of a powerful simile: "He was in such agony and he prayed so fervently that his sweat became like drops of blood falling on the ground" (22:44). This does not say that he literally sweat blood—it says that his sweat was so great that when it fell it was like drops of blood. This is the perspiration of a great athlete, locked in a wrestling match he dare not lose, giving the match everything he has, to the point that his sweat might as well be his blood. This is Jesus, ultimately wrestling not with temptation, but embracing his own acceptance of what lies ahead in the next few hours. His prayer is heard in heaven and his will has been steeled by an angel to do what his Father has asked of him. Jesus will meet the challenge of the final test. But what about his disciples?

Having prayed and been strengthened for the agony that lies ahead, Jesus returns to his disciples and finds them sleeping. They have not been praying. Instead of entering the agony of struggle against failure, they have fallen asleep from grief. When a loss becomes too great a burden to bear, the easiest way to shed the experience is simply to lose one's awareness in sleep. If the disciples are sleeping out of grief, they must sense that a betrayal is truly at hand and it means that Jesus has been serious all along in telling them, "The Son of Man must suffer greatly and be rejected by the elders, the chief priests, and the scribes, and be killed" (Luke 9:22).

Returning from his prayer, he asks them why they are sleeping and reminds them one last time to "pray that you may not undergo the test" (22:46). Jesus has committed himself to undergoing the test. Any struggle over making that commitment he has put into a permanent chokehold; it is only by Jesus' example, by fervent prayer and the assistance of the Holy Spirit, that disciples, then and now, will be delivered from the test.

## THE SECOND SORROWFUL MYSTERY
### The Scourging at the Pillar
*John 18:28–19·1*

²⁸Then they brought Jesus from Caiaphas to the praetorium. It was morning. And they themselves did not enter the praetorium, in order not to be defiled so that they could eat the Passover. ²⁹So Pilate came out to them and said, "What charge do you bring [against] this man?" ³⁰They answered and said to him, "If he were not a criminal, we would not have handed him over to you." ³¹At this, Pilate said to them, "Take him yourselves, and judge him according to your law." The Jews answered him, "We do not have the right to execute anyone," ³²in order that the word of Jesus might be fulfilled that he said indicating the kind of death he would die. ³³So Pilate went back into the praetorium and summoned Jesus and said to him, "Are you the King of the Jews?" ³⁴Jesus answered, "Do you say this on your own or have others told you about me?" ³⁵Pilate answered, "I am not a Jew, am I? Your own nation and the chief priests handed you over to me. What have you done?" ³⁶Jesus answered, "My kingdom does not belong to this world. If my kingdom did belong to this world, my attendants [would] be fighting to keep me from being handed over to the Jews. But as it is, my kingdom is not here." ³⁷So Pilate said to him, "Then you are a king?" Jesus answered, "You say I am a king. For this I was born and for this I came into the world, to testify to the truth. Everyone who belongs to the truth listens to my voice." ³⁸Pilate said to him, "What is truth?"

When he had said this, he again went out to the Jews and said to them, "I find no guilt in him. ³⁹But you have a custom that I release one prisoner to you at Passover. Do you want me to release to you the King of the Jews?" ⁴⁰They cried out again, "Not this one but Barabbas!" Now Barabbas was a revolutionary.

¹⁹·¹Then Pilate took Jesus and had him scourged.

In John's account, Jesus is scourged in the middle of Pilate's interrogation, rather than at its conclusion, as in Matthew (27:26) and Mark (15:15). Luke omits it altogether, but only after Pilate declares in two different places that he intends to limit Jesus' punishment to that of being scourged ("flogged," 23:16, 22). Scourging involves the lashing with a hard-tipped whip with several leather thongs. It is a cruel punishment inflicting great pain as it rips flesh into bloody strips. Our sorrow at Jesus' flogging is surprisingly at odds with John's account of it, however. Pilate's scourging of Jesus is presented by John not so much to provoke our sorrow or sympathy as to lay further claim on our faith. When read carefully, the faithful see in John's account that even in his trial and scourging, Jesus remained the one who is king in God's kingdom, the one who uniquely reveals the truth that is God. No human authority or power, whatever means of torture they possessed, could ever squelch the light of revelation that is Jesus' very person. Because of where John places the scourging, the trial itself has to be examined.

John has by far the longest description of Pilate's trial of Jesus. It is filled with drama and is an excellent example of John's skillful hand at weaving decades of theological reflection into his divinely inspired account of Jesus of Nazareth, the Word of God made flesh and the Light of the World.

Throughout John's gospel he has focused on specific encounters Jesus has with both individuals and groups of people. In all of these encounters, the characters involved are confronted with the necessity of accepting or rejecting Jesus as the one who has come down from heaven to fully reveal the Father. Jesus' trial and scourging in John is just such an encounter between Jesus and two principal characters. The first "character" is a group, the officials of the highest Jewish court, the Sanhedrin (who act as one) and the second is Pilate, who represents Rome itself. In John 18:28–19:1 the responses to Jesus by the highest officials of Judaism and the Roman state are given to heighten our awareness to the importance of recognizing Jesus as the fullness of God's revelation. They do nothing to tell us of the spiritual state of the Jews as people or secular authorities, then or now. In John's account, however, the Jewish authorities and Pilate do represent more than just themselves. They represent the self-serving blindness to which both institutional religion and political powers can freely lend themselves.

John's description of the Jewish authorities' behavior is damning. Even before Jesus appeared before Annas, the former high priest, and Caiaphas, the current high priest, the Sanhedrin had already determined that Jesus must die. Soon after Jesus raised his friend Lazarus from the dead (John 11:38-44), the Sanhedrin convened to discuss what to do with

Jesus. They feared so many of the people would proclaim him king, spelling rebellion to the Roman authorities, that Rome would then crush the entire nation. Caiaphas had provided the solution: "it is better for you that one man should die instead of the people, so that the whole nation may not perish" (John 11:50).

For John, the Sanhedrin authorities represent the crassest sort of rejection of Jesus possible. They know his works, that he has even raised someone from the dead. But rather than accept the truth that God was present in Jesus in a unique way, they choose to bring the author of life to a cruel death at the hands of the Romans because it seems politically expedient. In an act of ultimate hypocrisy, they bring Jesus to Pilate but refuse to step foot on the grounds of the praetorium lest they become defiled and unable to fully participate in the Passover. Unlike in the Synoptic Gospels, where the Passover had already been celebrated, in John the Passover will not take place until the approaching evening. John, then, is portraying the Jewish leaders as hypocrites. In the very act of following their religious purity rules surrounding the partaking of a lamb during Passover, they are personally sending the true Lamb of God to his death. And yet John tells us nothing about Jesus' appearance before Caiaphas, the highest official of the Sanhedrin. We are told only that "Annas sent him bound to Caiaphas the high priest." And then, after appearing before Caiaphas, "they brought Jesus from Caiaphas to the praetorium" (John 18:24, 28). The praetorium served as Pilate's headquarters only while he was in Jerusalem. His home base was actually far to the northwest of Jerusalem, at Caesaria Maritima, on the Mediterranean coast south of Mount Carmel. He was probably in Jerusalem because of the many pilgrims who had flocked there for the Passover.

Throughout the trial these Jewish officials will act as an impediment to Pilate, who appears to wish only to be rid of the whole affair, finding nothing worthy of crucifixion in Jesus' supposed offense. It is the obstinacy of the Jewish religious officials that ultimately forces Pilate to order Jesus' crucifixion. In showing us that, however, John also shows us that Jesus, being truth itself, rather than being tried by Pilate, puts Pilate and Roman authority on trial and finds them both wanting. While never freeing the Sanhedrin officials from blame, John wants our attention to focus on Pilate's interactions with Jesus.

Jesus never denies the Sanhedrin or Pilate their earthly powers, but they are both found wanting in their relationship to the truth. It is the truth that Jesus reveals that brings true freedom. As Jesus had proclaimed earlier in John, "If you remain in my word, you will truly be my disciples, and you will know the truth, and the truth will set you free" (8:31-32).

As soon as Jesus is handed over, Pilate makes it known that he is not under the thumbs of the Jewish officials. He represents Rome and will always act in his official capacity. He does this by asking, "What charge do you bring [against] this man?" (18:29). The question might have surprised the officials. In John, and only in John, we are told that among those who came out to arrest Jesus were soldiers. These could be no other than Roman soldiers officially assisting in Jesus' arrest. If Pilate, as the Roman prefect (governor) of Judea, had not authorized it, they could not have participated. He knows exactly why Jesus was arrested, but now, as judge, he must verify the charges and either punish or discharge the prisoner.

Pilate wants to know why the Sanhedrin didn't punish the prisoner using their own authority, and their answer says that the only fitting punishment they will consider is crucifixion. While they may or may not have had the authority to execute someone by stoning, only Roman authority had the power to execute by crucifixion. For John, this fulfills Jesus' own prediction that he will be crucified, meaning that however successful in their machinations against Jesus, it is Jesus who is in control; they cannot but fulfill Jesus' prophecy (18:32).

At the time Jesus was put on trial, Israel had been divided into several districts, all of them bound to Roman authority. Pilate's interrogation of Jesus focuses on the charge that Jesus regards himself as "the King of the Jews," and that as their king, he intends to rule a kingdom free of Rome's dominance. Such a kingdom would be possible only by revolting against Roman authority, which would make crucifixion the appropriate sentence. The spiritual importance of this interrogation and Pilate's attempt to release Jesus will be examined in greater detail in "The Crowning with Thorns," the third sorrowful mystery.

Here, it only need be noted that Pilate, while finding no guilt in Jesus, bows to pressure from the Sanhedrin officials and has Jesus flogged. Jesus is then scorned and mocked by Pilate's soldiers (not Herod's, as in Luke 23:11), but all who read of it in John know that the mockery of these soldiers is actually a proclamation of the truth: Jesus is King.

## THE THIRD SORROWFUL MYSTERY

### The Crowning with Thorns

*John 18:28–19:5*

[28]Then they brought Jesus from Caiaphas to the praetorium. It was morning. And they themselves did not enter the praetorium, in order not to be defiled so that they could eat the Passover. [29]So Pilate came out to them and said, "What charge do you bring [against] this man?" [30]They answered and said to him, "If he were not a criminal, we would not have handed him over to you." [31]At this, Pilate said to them, "Take him yourselves, and judge him according to your law." The Jews answered him, "We do not have the right to execute anyone," [32]in order that the word of Jesus might be fulfilled that he said indicating the kind of death he would die. [33]So Pilate went back into the praetorium and summoned Jesus and said to him, "Are you the King of the Jews?" [34]Jesus answered, "Do you say this on your own or have others told you about me?" [35]Pilate answered, "I am not a Jew, am I? Your own nation and the chief priests handed you over to me. What have you done?" [36]Jesus answered, "My kingdom does not belong to this world. If my kingdom did belong to this world, my attendants [would] be fighting to keep me from being handed over to the Jews. But as it is, my kingdom is not here." [37]So Pilate said to him, "Then you are a king?" Jesus answered, "You say I am a king. For this I was born and for this I came into the world, to testify to the truth. Everyone who belongs to the truth listens to my voice." [38]Pilate said to him, "What is truth?"

When he had said this, he again went out to the Jews and said to them, "I find no guilt in him. [39]But you have a custom that I release one prisoner to you at Passover. Do you want me to release to you the King of the Jews?" [40]They cried out again, "Not this one but Barabbas!" Now Barabbas was a revolutionary.

[19:1]Then Pilate took Jesus and had him scourged. [2]And the soldiers wove a crown out of thorns and placed it on his head, and clothed him in a purple cloak, [3]and they came to him and said, "Hail, King of the Jews!" And they struck him repeatedly. [4]Once more Pilate went out and said to them, "Look, I am bringing him out to you, so that you may know that I find no guilt in him." [5]So Jesus came out, wearing the crown of thorns and the purple cloak. And he said to them, "Behold, the man!"

In all four gospels, Jesus knows that his life will end on a cross. It is the inevitable result of faithfulness to his mission. Unlike any of the other gospels, however, John never depicts Jesus' crucifixion as a tragedy. Those who conspired together to have him put to death are surely villains in John's gospel, but what they don't realize is that they have conspired to fulfill Jesus' plan to reveal God's love. Jesus' arrest, the subsequent trial by Pontius Pilate, and the whipping and mockery he endures succeed only in further revealing who Jesus is and why he has come into the world. Jesus even regards his forthcoming crucifixion as a triumphant act: "'And when I am lifted up from the earth, I will draw everyone to myself.' He said this indicating the kind of death he would die" (John 12:32-33).

In John, every aspect of his passion, from his prayer after the Last Supper, to his arrest and trial, in his scourging at the pillar, and ultimately in his death on the cross, Jesus is not the victim, but the conqueror. Knowing of his imminent arrest, Jesus says of his forthcoming passion, "Now is the time of judgment on this world; now the ruler of this world will be driven out" (12:31). After Pilate has him scourged, when Jesus is crowned with thorns, dressed in a royal purple cloak, and mocked as a would-be king while being buffeted with blows, the readers of John know the truth. He is the King. He is our King.

Pilate's interrogation and Jesus' responses follow a typical Johannine pattern. Pilate's frame of reference is entirely secular, embedded in the political context of earthly human affairs. If Pilate had any inkling of who he was actually dealing with, he would realize that Jesus' responses are an invitation to awaken his inner self to a different, ultimate reality. Jesus is the head of a kingdom God has begun to plant into the world in the person of his Son. It isn't that Jesus' kingdom will attempt a violent secession from the Roman Empire; rather, it will make the Roman world irrelevant in comparison. The world and all that is in it belongs to God (Deut 10:14) and God, in Jesus, has set about taking it back.

Pilate is savvy enough, however, to realize that Jesus is no threat to Rome. When Pilate asks Jesus directly, "Then you are a king?" (18:37a), Jesus' response proves to him that Jesus and the so-called kingdom he belongs to are irrelevant to Rome. Jesus says nothing of military power or followers bent on either victory or martyrdom. "My kingdom does not belong to this world. If my kingdom did belong to this world, my attendants [would] be fighting to keep me from being handed over to the Jews. But as it is, my kingdom is not here" (18:36).

The authority Jesus has as a king means nothing to Pilate. Pilate need hear no more from Jesus. His talk of truth is mere words, certainly not the stuff of revolt or insurrection. In response, Pilate is dismissive of Jesus and whatever he might actually represent. "Pilate said to him, 'What is truth?'" (18:38).

Certain that Jesus is probably no more than a spouter of some home-grown Jewish philosophy, Pilate attempts to set him free by offering him to the Sanhedrin officials as a Passover amnesty. Who would the Jewish leaders regard as a greater threat to their own peaceful relations with Rome—this philosopher, or a true insurrectionist, Barabbas? Pilate's offer is couched in words that mock the Jewish people, yet actually proclaim the truth about Jesus. "Do you want me to release to you the King of the Jews?" (18:39). Pilate fails in his plan to free Jesus; the leaders choose the true insurrectionist. By the time this gospel was written (AD 90–100), Jerusalem and its temple had been crushed (AD 70) following an actual insurrection. The Sanhedrin and its officials ceased to exist.

Pilate has Jesus scourged. His soldiers robe him as a king beneath a crown of thorns and, thus garbed, Pilate parades him before the Jewish officials. "Behold the man!" he tells them. Once again, John uses words that function on two radically different levels.

We might pause at this point and remind ourselves of the prayerful question of Psalm 8:5—"What is man that you are mindful of him, / and a son of man that you care for him?"—and draw from Genesis an answer:

> Then God said: Let us make human beings in our image, after our likeness. Let them have dominion over the fish of the sea, the birds of the air, the tame animals, all the wild animals, and all the creatures that crawl on the earth.
> God created mankind in his image;
>> in the image of God he created them;
>> male and female he created them. (Gen 1:26-27)

That human beings are created in the image of God is the foundation for belief in human dignity for both Judaism and Christianity. Christian theologians have long attempted to elaborate a conceptual understanding of what it is about humans that qualify us as the image of God. Immortality of the soul, the self-awareness of human consciousness, our creative capacities, and, would that it were more evident, our capacity to love selflessly are considered.

From the time the Old Testament first began to be put into writing, right up through the New Testament period, there was a common practice throughout most of the empires of the biblical world: Kings and emperors were thought of as children of the reigning gods of the local pantheons. This was even true in Israel. Psalm 2 is a royal psalm, a psalm that was prayed for a new king upon his ascension to the throne. It was a moment when his subjects believed he became an adopted son of God.

Kings, as adopted sons of gods, would have their images, which were also statues of the god they represented, placed throughout their realms to remind their subjects to whom they owed their loyalty. When Genesis 1:26-27 speaks of God creating man and woman in the image of God, the message is that we were created to be kings and queens, to behave in the world and act toward all of creation as special representatives of the Creator, the one who knows and loves the goodness of everything created. We are to represent the love of God, the justice of God, the mercy of God.

"Behold the man!" The pathetic, beaten, bruised, and bleeding man. "Is this the king you so feared?" is what Pilate seems to be proclaiming. John, however, knows the truth he is proclaiming to us: "Behold the Man, the image of God, the Son of God who has come in the flesh to redeem us." Beaten, bruised, and bleeding beneath a crown of thorns, this is our God, standing in our midst. We see him as thus in adults and children, male and female, on our televisions, on our smartphones, in images from around the world, and even on our street corners or hiding behind the doors of our neighbors' houses.

## THE FOURTH SORROWFUL MYSTERY

### Jesus Carries His Cross

*Mark 15:20-23*

> [20]And when they had mocked him, they stripped him of the purple cloak, dressed him in his own clothes, and led him out to crucify him.
>
> [21]They pressed into service a passer-by, Simon, a Cyrenian, who was coming in from the country, the father of Alexander and Rufus, to carry his cross.
>
> [22]They brought him to the place of Golgotha (which is translated Place of the Skull). [23]They gave him wine drugged with myrrh, but he did not take it.

## Matthew 27:31-34

<sup>31</sup>And when they had mocked him, they stripped him of the cloak, dressed him in his own clothes, and led him off to crucify him.

<sup>32</sup>As they were going out, they met a Cyrenian named Simon; this man they pressed into service to carry his cross.

<sup>33</sup>And when they came to a place called Golgotha (which means Place of the Skull), <sup>34</sup>they gave Jesus wine to drink mixed with gall. But when he had tasted it, he refused to drink.

## Luke 23:26-32

<sup>26</sup>As they led him away they took hold of a certain Simon, a Cyrenian, who was coming in from the country; and after laying the cross on him, they made him carry it behind Jesus. <sup>27</sup>A large crowd of people followed Jesus, including many women who mourned and lamented him. <sup>28</sup>Jesus turned to them and said, "Daughters of Jerusalem, do not weep for me; weep instead for yourselves and for your children, <sup>29</sup>for indeed, the days are coming when people will say, 'Blessed are the barren, the wombs that never bore and the breasts that never nursed.' <sup>30</sup>At that time people will say to the mountains, 'Fall upon us!' and to the hills, 'Cover us!' <sup>31</sup>for if these things are done when the wood is green what will happen when it is dry?" <sup>32</sup>Now two others, both criminals, were led away with him to be executed.

## John 19:16b-17

<sup>16b</sup>So they took Jesus, <sup>17</sup>and carrying the cross himself he went out to what is called the Place of the Skull, in Hebrew, Golgotha.

In every gospel except John, the context makes it clear that those who take Jesus to be crucified are Roman soldiers. While the context in John might seem to imply that the "they" who took Jesus are the Jewish authorities, at the actual scene of the crucifixion John makes it clear that Roman soldiers are in charge (19:23). Matthew closely follows Mark's account of Jesus' journey from the praetorium to Golgotha, "the Place of the Skull," where he will be crucified. The minor differences, however, have something interesting to tell us.

The soldiers spot one Simon, a Cyrenian, and "pressed" him to carry the cross for Jesus. Cyrene was a major city on the northeastern coast of what is now Libya. It did have a Jewish population and in Acts 11:20, Cyrenians are said to be among the first to proclaim the Gospel to Gentiles, which happened in Antioch.

Mark's identification of Simon as the father of Alexander and Rufus tells us that they were all known as fellow Christians to his audience (probably in Rome). These names appear elsewhere in the New Testament but no one can say with conviction that they refer to the same individuals. That the sons' names are not mentioned by Matthew tells us their names were of no significance to his community, but Simon's name had become firmly embedded in Christian memory.

Nothing in Mark or Matthew's accounts describes Simon as a disciple of Jesus at the time he is pressed into carrying his cross, but Luke's careful wording, "they made him carry it behind Jesus," paints the mental picture of Simon *following* Jesus, and following Jesus is what a disciple does. In Luke, discipleship can occur immediately, as quickly as one might begin to follow Jesus. And what does it mean to follow Jesus? "If anyone wishes to come after me, he must deny himself and take up his cross daily and follow me" (Luke 9:23). We will see another instant discipleship occur in Luke when we meet the repentant thief at the crucifixion.

Mark has Simon "coming in from the country" when the soldiers grab him. Matthew doesn't mention this, and some have speculated that Matthew understood Simon to be a Jew and that Sabbath laws forbidding travel would be in place on what he considers Passover morning.

John makes no mention of Simon. John does not allow that anyone other than Jesus carried the cross: "and carrying the cross himself he went out to what is called the Place of the Skull" (19:17). What are we to make of this discrepancy? John may have had theological reasons for not mentioning Simon. In John 10:17-18, Jesus says, "This is why the Father loves me, because I lay down my life in order to take it up again. No one takes it from me, but I lay it down on my own. I have power to lay it down, and power to take it up again." John wants us to be fully aware that Jesus is no helpless victim on his way to his crucifixion. He is in charge because he is doing his Father's will.

Many have attempted to harmonize John with the Synoptic Gospels. One attempt suggests Jesus carried the horizontal crossbeam and that Simon carried the post to which it would later be attached. Roman historical accounts of crucifixions, however, consistently describe the victim as carrying the horizontal beam to a post that has already been set in place. Another attempt at harmonization suggests that Jesus carried his cross as far as he could, but after falling from weakness from his scourging, Simon was pressed into service. While Roman historical accounts also describe the one condemned carrying his own crossbeam, should Christ at any point have been so weakened that he was physically incapable of carrying his cross, pressing Simon into carrying it for him, wouldn't seem unlikely. Raymond Brown (the late Johannine scholar of note) states that Jesus was the first Jew in the first century for which there is any record of the Romans crucifying. We cannot say for certain what Roman protocol concerning crucifixions in Israel dictated at that time.

We should not read into John's statement (19:17), "carrying the cross himself [Jesus] went out to what is called the Place of the Skull," he meant to allow for the possibility that someone else would help Jesus carry his cross further along the way. Even if that were what happened, any historical plausibility must give way to John's theology in this matter: Jesus is taking up his own cross. He would not be going to his crucifixion if he were doing anything other than fulfilling the will of his Father.

Jesus' total acceptance of his imminent death is also found in Matthew 26:53-54. After one of his disciples tries to stop Jesus' arrest by using a sword, Jesus tells him, "Do you think that I cannot call upon my Father and he will not provide me at this moment with more than twelve legions of angels? But then how would the scriptures be fulfilled which say that it must come to pass in this way?"

Luke gives us the most details about Jesus' journey to the Place of the Skull, and in his account we are again confronted with a Savior that is determined to make that journey. He allows no pity for himself, because his own death is but a small sample of what lies ahead for the people of Jerusalem. In Matthew, from the time of his trial on, Jesus encounters only rejection and repudiation. There are crowds of people who cry out for his crucifixion and they even call down upon themselves and their children responsibility for his death (Matt 27:23-25). There is also a large crowd in Luke, but among them are "many women who mourned and lamented him" (23:27). Some scholars see these women as fulfilling a civic duty to mourn fellow Jews facing execution for which they may even have been paid, but in their culture that would not have created any doubts about their expressions of grief.

Far from questioning their grief, Jesus warns the women to withhold their tears, for a time of untold sorrow for themselves and their own children was coming (23:28-30). Jesus knew that the people of Jerusalem would eventually be crushed by the Romans. During his triumphal entry into Jerusalem just days before his arrest, Jesus himself had wept for Jerusalem:

> As he drew near, he saw the city and wept over it, saying, "If this day you only knew what makes for peace—but now it is hidden from your eyes. For the days are coming upon you when your enemies will raise a palisade against you; they will encircle you and hem you in on all sides. They will smash you to the ground and your children within you, and they will not leave one stone upon another within you because you did not recognize the time of your visitation." (Luke 19:41-44)

This is an accurate description of what Jerusalem experienced in AD 70 following a massive revolt against Rome by the Jewish people. Jesus, heading directly to his crucifixion, warns the women that his death was happening "when the wood is green." What, then, might they expect when it is dry? The analogy he offered supplies the image of firewood. If moist, green wood can be consumed so easily, what will happen when the wood has all become dry as kindling? It will bring about a fulfillment of a prophecy found in Hosea: "Then they will cry out to the mountains, 'Cover us!' / and to the hills, 'Fall upon us!'" (Hos 10:8).

In providing us with this encounter with the grieving daughters of Jerusalem, Luke was also demonstrating Jesus' unfaltering love for his people, showing us that to the very end he grieved that so many had not embraced his call to enter the kingdom of God. In telling us that "two others, both criminals, were led away with him to be executed" (23:32), Luke is preparing us for Jesus' final, successful offering of forgiveness and entry into the kingdom of God.

## THE FIFTH SORROWFUL MYSTERY

### The Crucifixion

*John 19:16-35*

> [16]Then he handed him over to them to be crucified.
>
> So they took Jesus, [17]and carrying the cross himself he went out to what is called the Place of the Skull, in Hebrew, Golgotha. [18]There they crucified him, and with him two others, one on either side, with Jesus in the middle. [19]Pilate also had an inscription written and put on the cross. It read, "Jesus the Nazorean, the King of the Jews."

²⁰Now many of the Jews read this inscription, because the place where Jesus was crucified was near the city; and it was written in Hebrew, Latin, and Greek. ²¹So the chief priests of the Jews said to Pilate, "Do not write 'The King of the Jews,' but that he said, 'I am the King of the Jews.'" ²²Pilate answered, "What I have written, I have written."

²³When the soldiers had crucified Jesus, they took his clothes and divided them into four shares, a share for each soldier. They also took his tunic, but the tunic was seamless, woven in one piece from the top down. ²⁴So they said to one another, "Let's not tear it, but cast lots for it to see whose it will be," in order that the passage of scripture might be fulfilled [that says]:

"They divided my garments among them,
    and for my vesture they cast lots."

This is what the soldiers did. ²⁵Standing by the cross of Jesus were his mother and his mother's sister, Mary the wife of Clopas, and Mary of Magdala. ²⁶When Jesus saw his mother and the disciple there whom he loved, he said to his mother, "Woman, behold, your son." ²⁷Then he said to the disciple, "Behold, your mother." And from that hour the disciple took her into his home.

²⁸After this, aware that everything was now finished, in order that the scripture might be fulfilled, Jesus said, "I thirst." ²⁹There was a vessel filled with common wine. So they put a sponge soaked in wine on a sprig of hyssop and put it up to his mouth. ³⁰When Jesus had taken the wine, he said, "It is finished." And bowing his head, he handed over the spirit.

³¹Now since it was preparation day, in order that the bodies might not remain on the cross on the sabbath, for the sabbath day of that week was a solemn one, the Jews asked Pilate that their legs be broken and they be taken down. ³²So the soldiers came and broke the legs of the first and then of the other one who was crucified with Jesus. ³³But when they came to Jesus and saw that he was already dead, they did not break his legs, ³⁴but one soldier thrust his lance into his side, and immediately blood and water flowed out. ³⁵An eyewitness has testified, and his testimony is true; he knows that he is speaking the truth, so that you also may [come to] believe.

Every gospel mentions the fact that Jesus was crucified along with two others. Matthew (27:38) and Mark (15:27) identify the other two as revolutionaries, Luke (23:32) refers to them as criminals. Only Luke tells us that one of them obtained a promise of salvation from Jesus (23:42-43).

John mentions them only in order to have them contrasted later with Jesus, when the soldiers break their legs in order to hasten their deaths.

The inscription placed on Jesus' cross renews John's exploration of the troubled relationship between Pilate and the Jewish priests (19:19-22). In the other gospels the inscription simply reads, "King of the Jews." John gives us an expanded inscription, one written not just in Hebrew (Aramaic), but also in Latin and Greek, each saying "Jesus the Nazorean, the King of the Jews." The Latin initials for this phrase, "INRI" (sometimes "JNRI"), are frequently found on crucifixes. John tells us that the inscription upset many Jews who read it, prompting the chief priests to ask Pilate to change it to "he said, 'I am the King of the Jews.'"

Pilate's answer, "What I have written, I have written," taunts the priests for having forced his hand in sentencing Jesus to death. Now he is asserting his authority by insisting on an indictment of Jesus that asserts Jesus had a claim to Jewish royalty. However spiteful Pilate's motives were, his ironic declaration of Jesus as King of the Jews in three languages foreshadows the spread of the Gospel throughout the Roman Empire. Pilate has unwittingly promoted the truth he shrugged off during his interrogation of Jesus (John 18:18).

Matthew (27:35), Mark (15:24), and Luke (23:34) tell us that the soldiers divided his garments after crucifying Jesus, but, once again, John has something special to tell us about the event. First, John makes sure we understand that the soldiers' act is a fulfillment of Scripture (Ps 22:19), but then John notifies us of something special among Jesus' garments—a tunic with no seam, woven in one piece so that it would have to be torn apart if it were to be divided. Most scholars believe this garment had symbolic significance for John. What might the spiritual significance of this seamless garment be?

Many suggestions have been made over the ages, not one of which has proven to be definitive. We do well to remind ourselves that symbols can have more than one meaning. Among those that Raymond Brown found most creditable are the suggestions that, above all, the seamless garment represents the unity of the church. It was of extreme importance to Jesus that his followers remain united in the bond of love (see John 10:16; 11:51-52; 13:34-35; 17:11, 20-21). Brown and others find it quite possible that John's description of the seamless garment was symbolic of the special robe worn by the high priests of the temple (Exod 28:4; Lev 16:4). While not specifically described as seamless in the Bible, the first-century (AD) Jewish historian Josephus wrote that the High Priest's tunic was woven without seams. If John meant for this association, he would be telling us that Jesus' death not only exalted him (lifted him up) as king, but also that Jesus was the High Priest in his own sacrificial death. Elsewhere, the non-Johannine letter to the Hebrews clearly proclaims Jesus' role as our High Priest (8:1-2).

John tells us that not every one of Jesus' followers deserted him at the cross. Most Bible translations tell us that there were four women with him, including his mother and Mary Magdalene, as well as the disciple "whom he loved" (19:26). This disciple is traditionally believed to be John Zebedee, who tradition also credits with being the human author of the Fourth Gospel, though the gospel itself never identifies the Beloved Disciple by name. One reason may be that the author wants every Christian to identify with this disciple. This would make it especially poignant for us to hear Jesus, just moments before his death, tell his mother and the disciple whom he loved that they now belong to each other as mother and child.

In Jesus' declaration, "Woman, behold, your son," we hear for only the second time his referring to his mother as "woman." The first time was at the wedding at Cana, when Mary advised him that the host was running out of wine. His response was cryptic: "Woman, how does your concern affect me? My hour has not yet come" (John 2:4). In John 12:23, Jesus knows that he will soon be arrested and put to death, and his death is his "hour": "The hour has come for the Son of Man to be glorified." Now that his hour has come, he once again calls his mother "woman" and many Catholic scholars recognize in this that he is associating his mother with the original woman, the one who was named Eve because she was the mother of all the living (Gen 3:20). Mary and the Beloved Disciple are the mother and child of a new family, in the new creation (the church, see 2 Cor 5:17) brought about by Christ on the cross.

Jesus says that he thirsts, in order to fulfill Scripture. The Scripture intended is probably Psalm 22:16: "As dry as a potsherd is my throat; / my tongue cleaves to my palate; / you lay me in the dust of death." If so, it is interesting that this is the same psalm that begins, "My God, my God, why have you abandoned me?"—which Matthew (27:46) and Mark (15:34) tell us Jesus cried out from the cross. John does not include this among Jesus' last words, but many scholars tell us that when Jesus uttered the opening of Psalm 22 he would have done so with the entire psalm in his heart. Psalm 22 ends by proclaiming God's salvation: "The generation to come will be told of the Lord, / that they may proclaim to a people yet unborn / the deliverance you have brought" (v. 32).

Jesus is offered sour wine to drink from a sponge attached to a sprig of hyssop. Centuries earlier, the Israelites used hyssop to sprinkle blood on the lintels of their doors at the first Passover. Immediately after accepting the sour wine, Jesus utters his last words before dying: "It is finished." It is understood to be a cry of victory. Jesus has completed the work of salvation. Then, with his last breath, "he handed over the spirit" (19:30). In Luke, Jesus commends his spirit to his Father and dies (23:46). John implies something more as well. Jesus is symbolically handing over the Holy Spirit to the church (the women and the Beloved Disciple) attending him at the cross. He will do so literally by breathing on his disciples after he has risen from the dead (John 20:22).

Jesus, "the Lamb of God, who takes away the sin of the world" (John 1:29), dies on preparation day, the day before the Passover, on which the Passover lambs are sacrificed in the temple. In an apparent accommodation to Jewish sensibilities, the bodies of the crucified are to be taken down before sunset, which will be the beginning of Passover. To hasten their death the soldiers break the legs of the two crucified beside Jesus, but finding Jesus already dead, a soldier lances his side. Ancient and modern scholars say that the water and blood that flow out from Jesus are the certain signs that Jesus' death (his blood) imbues the waters of baptism with the Holy Spirit. This belief is given with ample assurance: "An eyewitness has testified, and his testimony is true; he knows that he is speaking the truth, so that you also may [come to] believe" (John 19:35).

# CHAPTER 4

# The Glorious Mysteries

## THE FIRST GLORIOUS MYSTERY

### The Resurrection

*Mark 16:1-8*

> ¹When the sabbath was over, Mary Magdalene, Mary, the mother of James, and Salome bought spices so that they might go and anoint him. ²Very early when the sun had risen, on the first day of the week, they came to the tomb. ³They were saying to one another, "Who will roll back the stone for us from the entrance to the tomb?" ⁴When they looked up, they saw that the stone had been rolled back; it was very large. ⁵On entering the tomb they saw a young man sitting on the right side, clothed in a white robe, and they were utterly amazed. ⁶He said to them, "Do not be amazed! You seek Jesus of Nazareth, the crucified. He has been raised; he is not here. Behold the place where they laid him. ⁷But go and tell his disciples and Peter, 'He is going before you to Galilee; there you will see him, as he told you.'" ⁸Then they went out and fled from the tomb, seized with trembling and bewilderment. They said nothing to anyone, for they were afraid.

Very few Christians have ever found Mark 16:1-8 to be a satisfying conclusion to the gospel or a sufficient account of the resurrection. There are several perceived problems with it. Most glaring of all is its abrupt ending. How could Mark have ended his account of the resurrection with women fleeing from Jesus' empty tomb in a state of fear and bewilderment? Also, the women have not actually encountered the risen Christ. They see that the tomb is empty, and a mysterious stranger tells them that Jesus has been raised and that they are to tell Peter and the other disciples to meet the risen Jesus in Galilee. But the message apparently never gets conveyed! The women are so stricken with fear that they tell no one. That does not jive with the account itself, however, for Mark has written down what they saw and heard.

From the earliest times up to the present, church leaders and Christian scholars have expressed the opinion that the original and complete conclusion to Mark's gospel must somehow have been lost. Perhaps a lamp fell on the open scroll of the original, before any copies were made, or the end might even have been torn off for reasons reprehensible or accidental. It is no accident, however, that very early on scribes attempted to rectify the matter by providing alternative endings to Mark's gospel. There are three that are often printed in modern English translations of the Bible. One, the so-called "Longer Ending," is considered canonical, that is, it is considered divinely inspired Scripture, but it is not regarded as actually belonging to the original Gospel of Mark. It usually appears as verses 9 through 20 of Mark 16.

## Mark 16:9-20

[9When he had risen, early on the first day of the week, he appeared first to Mary Magdalene, out of whom he had driven seven demons. 10She went and told his companions who were mourning and weeping. 11When they heard that he was alive and had been seen by her, they did not believe.

12After this he appeared in another form to two of them walking along on their way to the country. 13They returned and told the others; but they did not believe them either.

14[But] later, as the eleven were at table, he appeared to them and rebuked them for their unbelief and hardness of heart because they had not believed those who saw him after he had been raised. 15He said to them, "Go into the whole world and proclaim the gospel to every creature. 16Whoever believes and is baptized will be saved; whoever does not believe will be condemned. 17These signs will accompany those who believe: in my name they will drive out demons, they will speak new languages. 18They will pick up serpents [with their hands], and if they drink any deadly thing, it will not harm them. They will lay hands on the sick, and they will recover."

> ¹⁹So then the Lord Jesus, after he spoke to them, was taken up into heaven and took his seat at the right hand of God. ²⁰But they went forth and preached everywhere, while the Lord worked with them and confirmed the word through accompanying signs.]

This "Longer Ending" clears up a lot of concerns that arise from having Mark end at verse 16:8. In many ways it shows an awareness of how John 20 and Luke 24 reported the resurrection.

In recent times, New Testament scholars have given much more attention to the Gospel of Mark because of a general consensus among scholars that Mark was the first gospel to have been written down, and that Matthew and Luke owe a great deal of their content to Mark. Mark received less attention in the past because almost everything in it could be found in Matthew and Luke, which seemed to mean that they had more to offer both faithful and studious readers.

With renewed interest in Mark, scholars began to ask what nuances can be found in Mark that Matthew or Luke left out or changed. One particular dimension of Mark that did not carry over in all its sharpness was the way the disciples in Mark are so frequently portrayed in a negative light (see 4:13, 40; 6:52; 8:17-21, 32; 9:32; 10:32, 38). The consistent emphasis in Mark is that the disciples failed to comprehend the necessity of the cross to Jesus' mission. For example, in Mark 4:40, where Jesus accuses his disciples of being persons without faith, during the incident in Matthew 8:26, the accusation has been toned down. The disciples are called people of "little faith."

Mark's critical treatment of the disciples may be a reflection of his awareness of a difficulty confronting his own Christian community some thirty or more years after the resurrection. Because of persecution, Christians in Mark's community were probably being far less public about their faith. Some, perhaps, were even denying their faith in public while trying to claim it in private. One noted Catholic scholar of Mark's gospel, the late Eugene LaVerdiere, found a key to interpreting the entire gospel in Mark 1:1—"The beginning of the gospel of Jesus Christ [the Son of God]." LaVerdiere was certain that this was Mark's title for his gospel, a title that was as applicable to the conclusion of the gospel as it was to its first few words. In other words, Mark called his gospel "the beginning of the gospel" because the entire gospel, from its first word to its last, was only the beginning of the gospel. The gospel of Jesus Christ, the Son of God, had only just begun with the disciples, and after Jesus' death and resurrection, Jesus' disciples had only just begun to be faithful followers of Jesus, because only then did they embrace the necessity of Jesus' death and resurrection.

With LaVerdiere's interpretation in mind, it is possible to see in the original ending of Mark's gospel a well-intended conclusion. Out of fear and bewilderment, the women fail to tell anyone about the resurrection. Mark's community, however, knows that that is also their own situation. They know, in fact, that the women in Mark's gospel eventually reported what they had witnessed to the apostles and the apostles subsequently returned to Galilee, where it all began, where they were first called to follow Jesus. And there, after having their own encounter with the risen Christ, they began anew to follow him. That was how the gospel begins, not how it ends. The gospel begins when we take up our cross and follow Jesus.

## John 20:11-18

¹¹Mary stayed outside the tomb weeping. And as she wept, she bent over into the tomb ¹²and saw two angels in white sitting there, one at the head and one at the feet where the body of Jesus had been. ¹³And they said to her, "Woman, why are you weeping?" She said to them, "They have taken my Lord, and I don't know where they laid him." ¹⁴When she had said this, she turned around and saw Jesus there, but did not know it was Jesus. ¹⁵Jesus said to her, "Woman, why are you weeping? Whom are you looking for?" She thought it was the gardener and said to him, "Sir, if you carried him away, tell me where you laid him, and I will take him." ¹⁶Jesus said to her, "Mary!" She turned and said to him in Hebrew, "Rabbouni," which means Teacher. ¹⁷Jesus said to her, "Stop holding on to me, for I have not yet ascended to the Father. But go to my brothers and tell them, 'I am going to my Father and your Father, to my God and your God.'" ¹⁸Mary of Magdala went and announced to the disciples, "I have seen the Lord," and what he told her.

Anyone who carefully reads the resurrection accounts in each of the four gospels (Matt 28:1-20; Mark 16:1-8 [and vv. 9-20]; Luke 24:1-53; John 20:1–21:25) becomes aware that there are considerable differences between them. At the core of each one, however, are definite similarities. Each one tells of the empty tomb and each gospel tells us that women who had been followers of Jesus were the first to witness the empty tomb. The names and number of the women vary, but one is always mentioned, Mary of Magdala (Mary Magdalene). In the Gospel of John, we learn that she was the very first of Jesus' followers to encounter the risen Christ and also the very first person (other than an angel) to report the Good News of the resurrection. Because of this, Mary Magdalene has rightly been called "the apostle to the apostles."

But there is a bigger story concerning all the women who came to the empty tomb and bore witness to the resurrection. For much of Christian history, those who have scoffed at the resurrection often felt they had powerful ammunition to refute Christian belief in the resurrection, ammunition that they took from the gospel accounts. Their unanimity in recording that the first witnesses were women was seen as discrediting their reports. For much of history, women were believed to be unreliable witnesses. For example, only male witnesses could be used in Jewish courts in biblical times.

This discrediting of women was a flaw the apostles seemed to share with their times. In Luke's resurrection account Mary Magdalene and the other women try to tell the apostles what they witnessed at the empty tomb, "but their story seemed like nonsense and they did not believe them" (24:11). History has a way of righting things, however. That the gospels consistently count women as the first witnesses to the resurrection, in spite of the fact that the surrounding culture scoffed at women as witnesses, bears wonderful witness to the accuracy of the claim. If the women truly hadn't been the first witnesses—if the resurrection accounts were imaginative inventions—the gospels would never have made women the first witnesses. We believe in the risen Christ, and every Christian is indebted to the women who bore him faithful witness.

## THE SECOND GLORIOUS MYSTERY

### The Ascension

*Luke 24:44-53*

> [44]He said to them, "These are my words that I spoke to you while I was still with you, that everything written about me in the law of Moses and in the prophets and psalms must be fulfilled." [45]Then he opened their minds to understand the scriptures. [46]And he said to them, "Thus it is written that the Messiah would suffer and rise from the dead on the third day [47]and that repentance, for the for-

giveness of sins, would be preached in his name to all the nations, beginning from Jerusalem. [48]You are witnesses of these things. [49]And [behold] I am sending the promise of my Father upon you; but stay in the city until you are clothed with power from on high."

[50]Then he led them [out] as far as Bethany, raised his hands, and blessed them. [51]As he blessed them he parted from them and was taken up to heaven. [52]They did him homage and then returned to Jerusalem with great joy, [53]and they were continually in the temple praising God.

## Acts 1:6-11

[6]When they had gathered together they asked him, "Lord, are you at this time going to restore the kingdom to Israel?" [7]He answered them, "It is not for you to know the times or seasons that the Father has established by his own authority. [8]But you will receive power when the holy Spirit comes upon you, and you will be my witnesses in Jerusalem, throughout Judea and Samaria, and to the ends of the earth." [9]When he had said this, as they were looking on, he was lifted up, and a cloud took him from their sight. [10]While they were looking intently at the sky as he was going, suddenly two men dressed in white garments stood beside them. [11]They said, "Men of Galilee, why are you standing there looking at the sky? This Jesus who has been taken up from you into heaven will return in the same way as you have seen him going into heaven."

The resurrection, the ascension, and Pentecost are linked together so intimately that discussing the importance of one should inevitably lead to a discussion of the other two. The ascension, however, often gets treated as little more than a picturesque link between Easter and Pentecost. Today, influenced by modern astronomy, Luke's description of the ascension of our Lord in Acts (1:9b) gets discussed almost with quaint amusement because of this: "as they were looking on, he was lifted up, and a cloud took him from their sight." Indeed, as it is presented in Acts, attempts to visualize the ascension in a very literal fashion can seem bizarre. In some stained glass windows, the ascension is depicted with the disciples staring upward at a pair of nail-scarred feet sticking out from below a cloud.

There probably was a time when such depictions could speak to us with serious piety, but few of us are now able to stare up at the sky and wonder if heaven is literally a place somewhere up there, just behind

## Third Heaven

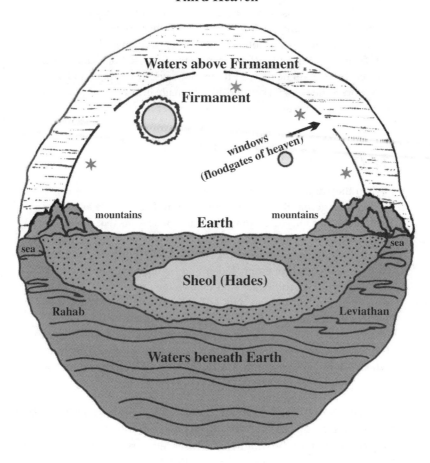

a cloud. In science, the study of the makeup of the universe—the cosmos—is called cosmology. Ancient biblical cosmology understood the structure of the universe far differently than we do today.

The earth was believed to rest above waters, and the sky with the sun, moon, and stars were thought of as the firmament, the first and lowest of three heavens. Above the firmament was another body of water, through the gates of which poured rain when they were opened by God. The uppermost heaven, the third heaven (see 2 Cor 12:2-4), was the paradise in which God and the angels dwelled. As Christians we do believe there is a heaven that is not of this earth, but today we can speak only of heaven as being "up there" in a metaphorical sense. We are probably closer to the truth when we attempt to speak or think of heaven as an ultimate reality, a dimension beyond the grasp of our senses but nevertheless a reality that is greater than anything we can encounter in the created order. Heaven is not so much "up" as it is beyond. But the three events of Jesus' resurrection, his ascension into heaven, and the outpouring of the Holy Spirit bring to us a bridge across that seemingly infinite gulf between an unreachable heaven and our life in this world.

This is not to say that the disciples didn't actually see Jesus "ascend" upwards at the ascension. That could have been a divine accommodation to the disciples that would help them ponder a great mystery. Jesus Christ, the Son of God, risen from the dead, is returning to his Father in heaven. What other way were they going to experience that? What is certainly true is that Luke thought there was no better way to describe Jesus' return to the Father.

The ascension is mentioned in John, but no description is given and John records it as happening right after the resurrection, before his appearances to any of the disciples other than Mary Magdalene. After seeing the empty tomb, Mary Magdalene has her encounter with her risen Lord.

## John 20:14-17

> [14][S]he turned around and saw Jesus there, but did not know it was Jesus. [15]Jesus said to her, "Woman, why are you weeping? Whom are you looking for?" She thought it was the gardener and said to him, "Sir, if you carried him away, tell me where you laid him, and I will take him." [16]Jesus said to her, "Mary!" She turned and said to him in Hebrew, "Rabbouni," which means Teacher. [17]Jesus said to her, "Stop holding on to me, for I have not yet ascended to the Father. But go to my brothers and tell them, 'I am going to my Father and your Father, to my God and your God.'"

There is something of real value to be gained by appreciating the differences between John and Luke in how they present the ascension. We will see something similar when we explore the descent of the Holy Spirit at Pentecost. John also presents the giving of the Holy Spirit quite differently than Luke presents it in Acts. In both instances, Luke's descriptions focus our attention on the events with graphic and dramatic detail. In Luke, the ascension occurs forty days after the resurrection. It is traditionally celebrated by the church on the Thursday ten days before Pentecost Sunday, but in the United States many churches celebrate it on the Sunday before Pentecost.

John describes the same events as intimate acts with much less fanfare. In John, the announcement of Jesus' imminent ascension is made only to Mary Magdalene, and she is told to stop clinging to him because his ascension is an intimate moment that will unite Jesus with the one who is both his Father and the Father of Jesus' disciples. As for the event itself, no disciple witnesses it; we are to simply assume that when Mary Magdalene obeyed Jesus and went to proclaim the Good News of the resurrection to Peter and the other disciples, Jesus ascended to his Father. John's concern is primarily to unite the three events of the resurrection, the ascension, and the giving of the Holy Spirit by presenting each of them as happening on Easter Sunday. Another difference is that for Luke, the ascension is a climactic event in Jesus' personal dealings with his disciples. Once he ascends to heaven he will not return to his disciples until the Second Coming.

> "Men of Galilee, why are you standing there looking at the sky? This Jesus who has been taken up from you into heaven will return in the same way as you have seen him going into heaven." (Acts 1:11)

In John, Jesus visits the disciples in the Upper Room on the same day, following his ascension to the Father. John's account invites us to consider the ascension as a necessary event that reunites the Son with his Father in a special way. The Word of God that came down from heaven has accomplished what he was sent into the world to do, to take away the sin of the world, and now is reunited with the Father in heaven. This does not prevent him from having further relations with his disciples. Even Luke will tell us that Jesus, sometime after his ascension, appeared to Saul of Tarsus as he was traveling to Damascus (Acts 9:1-6).

What John's account does for us is to encourage us to think of the resurrection, the ascension, and the outpouring of the Spirit as a triune Easter event. Each of them is inextricably united to the other as part of the salvation Jesus won for us on the cross.

John and Luke tell us of the ascension, but their accounts tug unceasingly on the imaginations of believers, saints, and theologians and over time they have reported many wonderful insights into its meaning. Because the incarnation is ongoing, because Jesus remains fully human, however glorified, after the resurrection, his ascension means that humanity, in Jesus, is now fully at home in the very heart of God. Because humanity now fully shares in the life of God, God can now come down to earth and live fully in the life of humanity. The ascension is in heaven what Pentecost is on earth. As Jesus united his humanity within the heart of God, God entered the heart of humanity united in Christ.

## THE THIRD GLORIOUS MYSTERY
### The Descent of the Holy Spirit
*Acts 2:1-8, 14-24*

[1]When the time for Pentecost was fulfilled, they were all in one place together. [2]And suddenly there came from the sky a noise like a strong driving wind, and it filled the entire house in which they were. [3]Then there appeared to them tongues as of fire, which parted and came to rest on each one of them. [4]And they were all filled with the holy Spirit and began to speak in different tongues, as the Spirit enabled them to proclaim.

[5]Now there were devout Jews from every nation under heaven staying in Jerusalem. [6]At this sound, they gathered in a large crowd, but they were confused because each one heard them speaking in his own language. [7]They were astounded, and in amazement they asked, "Are not all these people who are speaking Galileans? [8]Then how does each of us hear them in his own native language?" . . .

[14]Then Peter stood up with the Eleven, raised his voice, and proclaimed to them, "You who are Jews, indeed all of you staying in Jerusalem. Let this be known to you, and listen to my words. [15]These people are not drunk, as you suppose, for it is only nine o'clock in the morning. [16]No, this is what was spoken through the prophet Joel:

[17]'It will come to pass in the last days,' God says,
    'that I will pour out a portion of my spirit upon all flesh.
Your sons and your daughters shall prophesy,
    your young men shall see visions,
    your old men shall dream dreams.
[18]Indeed, upon my servants and my handmaids
    I will pour out a portion of my spirit in those days,
        and they shall prophesy.
[19]And I will work wonders in the heavens above
    and signs on the earth below:
        blood, fire, and a cloud of smoke.

<sup>20</sup>The sun shall be turned to darkness,
  and the moon to blood,
    before the coming of the great and splendid day of the Lord,
  <sup>21</sup>and it shall be that everyone shall be saved who calls on the
    name of the Lord.'

<sup>22</sup>You who are Israelites, hear these words. Jesus the Nazorean was a man commended to you by God with mighty deeds, wonders, and signs, which God worked through him in your midst, as you yourselves know. <sup>23</sup>This man, delivered up by the set plan and foreknowledge of God, you killed, using lawless men to crucify him. <sup>24</sup>But God raised him up, releasing him from the throes of death, because it was impossible for him to be held by it.

During the forty days between the resurrection and his ascension Jesus had been meeting with the eleven disciples and "speaking about the kingdom of God" (Acts 1:3). At his ascension Jesus told these apostles to remain in Jerusalem and await the baptism with the Holy Spirit (Acts 1:4-5). When the time arrives, it will be the fulfillment of what John prophesied about the one mightier than he who was to come after him, namely, Jesus: "He will baptize you with the holy Spirit and fire" (Luke 3:16). Having heard Jesus speak about the kingdom throughout these forty days, the apostles ask whether he will now restore the kingdom to Israel (Acts 1:6). Jesus' reply seems to suggest that the restoration of the kingdom was probably a long way off in telling them it was not for them to know the times or the seasons (Acts 1:7). Luke then proceeds to describe what happens immediately after the ascension and during the feast of Pentecost as initiating a restoration of the kingdom to Israel. Readers of Acts can be excused if they feel confused.

Faithful to Jesus' command, the apostles remain in Jerusalem, where they meet regularly with Jesus' mother and 120 other followers of Jesus. Under Peter's leadership the eleven apostles set about, through prayer and divination (the giving of lots, Acts 1:26), selecting Matthias to replace Judas as a twelfth apostle. This is a very important event in Luke's narrative. The necessity of replacing Judas was implied by the fact that Jesus chose the twelve apostles to rule over a renewed Israel:

It is you who have stood by me in my trials; and I confer a kingdom on you, just as my Father has conferred one on me, that you may eat and drink at my table in my kingdom; and you will sit on thrones judging the twelve tribes of Israel. (Luke 22:28-30)

In First Corinthians, Paul refers to the risen Christ having appeared to Cephas and "the Twelve," but aside from that single reference, and Luke's account in Acts, there is no other mention in the New Testament of a special retinue of twelve apostles following the resurrection. However, the importance of twelve tribes comprising God's people is attested to in the New Testament in James 1:1 and numerous places in Revelation (especially in association with the new Jerusalem).

There is no apparent distinction in Luke's two New Testament books (the gospel and Acts) between the kingdom of God and the kingdom that is to be restored to Israel. Luke set out to demonstrate that Jesus in his ministry, and the apostles in their continuation of Jesus' ministry, attempted to restore the kingdom to Israel through preaching, healing, and signs and wonders that accompanied them through the power of the Holy Spirit. Luke testifies that the apostles were quite successful at the beginning. Peter's Pentecostal address to the Jewish crowds visiting Jerusalem from afar for the feast led about three thousand to be baptized (Acts 2:41), and before long that number grew to five thousand men (Acts 4:4).

What is even more telling is that Luke clearly associates the descent of the Holy Spirit at Pentecost as an event associated with "the last days," that great Day of the Lord when God's rule will be made manifest not just in Israel, but throughout the earth. The events associated with the outpouring of the Spirit in Joel (2:14) are the signs and wonders of the end times:

> "And I will work wonders in the heavens above
> and signs on the earth below:
> blood, fire, and a cloud of smoke.
> The sun shall be turned to darkness,
> and the moon to blood,
> before the coming of the great and splendid day of the Lord,
> and it shall be that everyone shall be saved who calls on the name of
> the Lord." (Acts 2:19-21)

The outpouring of the Holy Spirit on Mary and the disciples gathered with the apostles is an inauguration of the kingdom of God on earth. For many generations Christians have rightly fixed their hope on the resurrection of the dead, which will be the crowning event of life in the kingdom of God, but as Peter preaches to the crowds, the resurrection of the dead has already begun—it is a reality in Jesus of Nazareth. The kingdom of God, then, is not only something that awaits us after death. The Christian understanding is that the mission of the church is and has been from the very beginning a Spirit-empowered endeavor to make a foretaste of God's kingdom a living reality in the world we live in.

Luke gives us a very dramatic portrayal of the outpouring of the Holy Spirit. He fixes its timing during the feast of Pentecost, which had come to be associated with the revelation of God at Sinai, but now something greater has occurred. The outpouring of the Spirit results in the immediate empowerment of the disciples who had just weeks before denied Jesus with oaths before others (Luke 22:54-60) and removed themselves at a distance at his crucifixion (Luke 23:49). They and the people to whom they bring the Good News of the resurrection will never be the same again.

John's description of the gift of the Holy Spirit is quite different. It is set at an earlier time, on that first Sunday in which Jesus rose from the dead. John describes it with far less drama, depicting it as an intimate moment between Jesus and his disciples. Rather than the revelation at Sinai, John associates the gift with the work of the Spirit at creation.

## *John 20:19-23*

> [19]On the evening of that first day of the week, when the doors were locked, where the disciples were, for fear of the Jews, Jesus came and stood in their midst and said to them, "Peace be with you." [20]When he had said this, he showed them his hands and his side. The disciples rejoiced when they saw the Lord. [21][Jesus] said to them again, "Peace be with you. As the Father has sent me, so I send you." [22]And when he had said this, he breathed on them and said to them, "Receive the holy Spirit. [23]Whose sins you forgive are forgiven them, and whose sins you retain are retained."

Compared to Luke's description of a noise like a strong driving wind that filled the entire house and tongues as of fire splitting and alighting on the disciples' heads, John's account seems calm, almost sedate. Indeed, it begins with Jesus greeting them with *Shalom aleichem*, that is, "Peace be with you" (20:19), and then he simply breathes on them. His words explain what he has just done for them, "Receive the holy Spirit" (20:22). God's breath first gave life to humanity (Gen 2:7), and it continually renews the life of every living thing (Ps 104:30). John's account is not so different from Luke's, however, in that the Spirit is a gift to the disciples flowing out of Christ's resurrection and it is the empowering of the disciples to proclaim the Good News of reconciliation with God for all who desire it (20:21-23).

Whether the Spirit comes upon us like fire, wind, or a peaceful breath, the gift is ours through baptism and confirmation and awaits renewal through prayer and penance. The responsorial psalm (104) during the Liturgy of the Word at Pentecost gracefully asks for this renewal: "Lord, send out your Spirit, and renew the face of the earth."

## THE FOURTH GLORIOUS MYSTERY

### The Assumption of Mary

*Revelation 11:19–12:10b*

11:19Then God's temple in heaven was opened, and the ark of his covenant could be seen in the temple. There were flashes of lightning, rumblings, and peals of thunder, an earthquake, and a violent hailstorm.

12:1A great sign appeared in the sky, a woman clothed with the sun, with the moon under her feet, and on her head a crown of twelve stars. 2She was with child and wailed aloud in pain as she labored to give birth. 3Then another sign appeared in the sky; it was a huge red dragon, with seven heads and ten horns, and on its heads were seven diadems. 4Its tail swept away a third of the stars in the sky and hurled them down to the earth. Then the dragon stood before the woman about to give birth, to devour her child when she gave birth. 5She gave birth to a son, a male child, destined to rule all the nations with an iron rod. Her child was caught up to God and his throne. 6The woman herself fled into the desert where she had a place prepared by God, that there she might be taken care of for twelve hundred and sixty days.

7Then war broke out in heaven; Michael and his angels battled against the dragon. The dragon and its angels fought back, 8but they did not prevail and there was no longer any place for them in heaven. 9The huge dragon, the ancient serpent, who is called the Devil and Satan, who deceived the whole world, was thrown down to earth, and its angels were thrown down with it.

10Then I heard a loud voice in heaven say:

"Now have salvation and power come,
    and the kingdom of our God
    and the authority of his Anointed.

> For the accuser of our brothers is cast out,
>   who accuses them before our God day and night."

The assumption of the Blessed Virgin, body and soul into heaven, is not an event ever mentioned in the Bible. It is, however, enshrined in sacred tradition and was officially recognized by the Catholic Church by an infallible declaration of Pope Pius XII in 1950. The Scripture most closely associated with her assumption is from the book of Revelation, and proclaimed during the Liturgy of the Word on the feast of the Assumption.

In Revelation 11:19, the heavenly Jerusalem is opened in a vision to one John, who never identifies himself as an apostle. In the vision, John beholds the ark of the covenant amidst "lightning, rumblings, and peals of thunder, an earthquake, and a violent hailstorm." These are apocalyptic signs—dramatic signs that accompany revelatory events. The ark of the covenant was kept in the holiest part of Jerusalem's first temple (Solomon's temple) and the stone tablets upon which were carved the Ten Commandments were kept inside the ark (1 Kgs 8:6-9). After the Babylonian army destroyed the temple in 586 BC there was never a verifiable record of its disposition. Second Maccabees 2:4 supplies a legend that the prophet Jeremiah took it with him when going into exile in Egypt after the Babylonian conquest, and hid it in a cave on Mount Sinai. Other legends suggest it was taken up into heaven.

This passage from Revelation is part of what is read at the liturgy for the feast of the Assumption because early Christian theologians regarded the original ark of the covenant as a sign that foreshadowed Mary's role in salvation history. When God sent his Son into the world as the new and eternal covenant with humanity, the presence of his Son in the world began in the womb of the Virgin Mary. Mary, then, could be said to be the "ark" within which the ultimate covenant was kept safe until his birth.

The identity of the woman "clothed with the sun, with the moon under her feet, and on her head a crown of twelve stars" is not something that can be absolutely associated with the Mother of our Lord, since she functions as a sign (a symbol) within a vision. On the other hand, as a sign, she cannot simply be disassociated from Mary either. The woman in the vision is certainly one with great dignity, as is suggested by her heavenly raiment, the crown of stars on her head with the moon serving as her footstool. Her identity is revealed within the spiritual drama in which she is engaged.

The woman is pregnant and crying out with labor pains. A seven-headed dragon with ten horns sweeps away a third of the stars from heaven and comes before the woman hoping to devour her child as soon as she gives birth. The child is clearly to be identified with Christ, for he is "destined to rule all the nations with an iron rod," and after he is born is "caught up to God and his throne." Here we see the drama of that great serpent, which Revelation 12:9 identifies as the devil and Satan, hoping to destroy Jesus, but his attempt is absolutely foiled when Christ, following the resurrection, ascends to the throne of heaven. It would seem quite natural to identify the woman, then, as Mary. What follows in this vision, however, tells us that the mother of the child, when pursued, is not herself caught up into heaven, but is taken to safety in the desert. There, the dragon pursues her but, foiled once again, turns instead to her other children whom he attempts to destroy (Rev 12:13-18).

These other children are what best help us identify who the woman symbolizes. The book of Revelation was written for a Christian audience in Asia Minor (what is now Turkey) during a time of official Roman persecution. Its intention was to supply courage to Christian communities variously struggling to remain true to their faith in spite of the persecution, which threatened them like the fiery breath of a dragon. John's vision of the woman, her child that was caught up into heaven, and the woman's other children whom the dragon sought to devour, painted a vivid picture of their predicament. Jesus was born into the same world as they were, died a horrible death at the hands of the same Roman persecutors, and then rose from the dead and ascended into heaven. They are to remain courageous in the face of death because their faith in Christ assures them of their own eventual resurrection should they be killed. They would have clearly understood that the woman who had also given them birth was the people of God, who had given them new birth in the waters of baptism.

The woman, then, is the mother of all the faithful as well as the mother of the Christ. It is impossible to dissociate the woman as a symbol from the real, physical mother who gave birth to Christ, and whom the Gospel of John portrays as a mother to Christ's disciples (19:26-27). Since the woman in Revelation is a sign (a symbol), however, she represents first of all the people of God as the maternal agency who brings forth all other brothers and sisters of Christ. There is a long and rich biblical tradition of representing God's people as a woman, "daughter Jerusalem" or "daughter Zion" (see Zeph 3:14; Zech 9:9).

The woman in Revelation 12, then, is a fitting reading to celebrate the assumption of the Virgin Mary, not because it is directly written about her or her assumption, but because it proclaims the great dignity of the mother of that child who was caught up into heaven. With her noble, heavenly regalia, we who believe in Mary's assumption are rightly reminded of her by that symbolic woman who was kept safe from the serpent and awaited her own resurrection.

At the crucifixion, Mary is depicted in John's gospel as being the new Eve, the new mother of the new creation. Stemming in part from that, the opposition in Revelation between the serpent and the woman often leads Christians to see in her another association with Mary, because of what God said in Genesis 3:15 concerning the serpent of Eden and Eve: "I will put enmity between you and the woman, / and between your offspring and hers; / They will strike at your head, / while you strike at their heel."

## 1 Corinthians 15:20-27a

> [20]But now Christ has been raised from the dead, the firstfruits of those who have fallen asleep. [21]For since death came through a human being, the resurrection of the dead came also through a human being. [22]For just as in Adam all die, so too in Christ shall all be brought to life, [23]but each one in proper order: Christ the firstfruits; then, at his coming, those who belong to Christ; [24]then comes the end, when he hands over the kingdom to his God and Father, when he has destroyed every sovereignty and every authority and power. [25]For he must reign until he has put all his enemies under his feet. [26]The last enemy to be destroyed is death, [27]for "he subjected everything under his feet."

The ultimate hope of all Christians is that we will share in Christ's resurrection. The faith of Catholics that Mary shared in her son's resurrection at the moment (or instant) of her death is grounded in our sacred tradition, not because it is revealed in Sacred Scripture. Nevertheless, Scripture is adamant that our hope of sharing in his resurrection is a genuine hope. His mother certainly hoped to share in his resurrection, for she is among his faithful disciples who first share in the outpouring of the Holy Spirt (Acts 1:14), which Paul calls the initial installment on our own resurrection (2 Cor 5:4-5). For Catholics, Mary's assumption further illuminates our hope and urges us on to greater faithfulness to the promise.

## THE FIFTH GLORIOUS MYSTERY

### The Crowning of the Blessed Virgin as Queen of Heaven and Earth

*Luke 1:26-28*

[26]In the sixth month, the angel Gabriel was sent from God to a town of Galilee called Nazareth, [27]to a virgin betrothed to a man named Joseph, of the house of David, and the virgin's name was Mary. [28]And coming to her, he said, "Hail, favored one! The Lord is with you."

*Luke 1:39-55*

[39]During those days Mary set out and traveled to the hill country in haste to a town of Judah, [40]where she entered the house of Zechariah and greeted Elizabeth. [41]When Elizabeth heard Mary's greeting, the infant leaped in her womb, and Elizabeth, filled with the holy Spirit, [42]cried out in a loud voice and said, "Most blessed are you among women, and blessed is the fruit of your womb. [43]And how does this happen to me, that the mother of my Lord should come to me? [44]For at the moment the sound of your greeting reached my ears, the infant in my womb leaped for joy. [45]Blessed are you who believed that what was spoken to you by the Lord would be fulfilled."

[46]And Mary said:

"My soul proclaims the greatness of the Lord;
   [47]my spirit rejoices in God my savior.
[48]For he has looked upon his handmaid's lowliness;
   behold, from now on will all ages call me blessed.
[49]The Mighty One has done great things for me,
   and holy is his name.
[50]His mercy is from age to age
   to those who fear him.
[51]He has shown might with his arm,
   dispersed the arrogant of mind and heart.
[52]He has thrown down the rulers from their thrones
   but lifted up the lowly.
[53]The hungry he has filled with good things;
   the rich he has sent away empty.
[54]He has helped Israel his servant,
   remembering his mercy,
[55]according to his promise to our fathers,
   to Abraham and to his descendants forever."

It may seem a bit strange to reflect on the coronation of Mary as Queen of Heaven and Earth by returning to Luke's unique accounts of the annunciation and Mary and Elizabeth's visitation. Her coronation, however, is not unlike the mystery of her assumption in that there is no text in Scripture that says anything about it. Sacred tradition, however, indisputably preserves her recognition as Queen of Heaven and Earth and in the Catholic Church's liturgy, celebrates her queenship with a specific feast on August 22 (originally May 31). The date of this feast, coming one week after the feast of the assumption, marks the close theological link between her assumption and her dignity as Queen of Heaven.

While few Christians outside Catholicism and Orthodoxy and some Anglicans venerate Mary in the same or similar fashion, it is in the visitation that we find the scriptural foundation for her veneration. We find it in the angel Gabriel's greeting, "Hail, favored one! The Lord is with you" (Luke 1:28b); and later on the lips of Elizabeth, "Most blessed are you among women, and blessed is the fruit of your womb" (Luke 1:42); and from Mary herself, "behold, from now on will all ages call me blessed" (Luke 1:48).

Scripture itself, however, makes it clear that Mary's blood relationship to Jesus is not the guarantor of a special relationship to God. It is Jesus himself that makes this clear.

> While he was speaking, a woman from the crowd called out and said to him, "Blessed is the womb that carried you and the breasts at which you nursed." He replied, "Rather, blessed are those who hear the word of God and observe it." (Luke 11:27-28)

Earlier in Luke, while Jesus was speaking to a large gathering, Mary and some of his relatives were anxious to talk to him, but Jesus seemingly does not even acknowledge his relationship to them:

> Then his mother and his brothers came to him but were unable to join him because of the crowd. He was told, "Your mother and your brothers are standing outside and they wish to see you." He said to them in reply, "My mother and my brothers are those who hear the word of God and act on it." (Luke 8:19-21)

It would be a mistake, however, to think Jesus was saying anything ill about his mother. Rather, his words define his true family, which is made up of those who hear the word of God and faithfully respond to it. It was central to Jesus' mission to call people into a new relationship with

God, a relationship that would also reorient them in their relationships with others. No one else in Luke has thus far embodied such attentive faithfulness as Mary.

On the one hand, those who wanted to follow Jesus had to be willing to reject their relationships to their family of origin, if those relationships prevented them from answering his call. "[E]veryone who has given up houses or brothers or sisters or father or mother or children or lands for the sake of my name will receive a hundred times more, and will inherit eternal life" (Matt 19:29). On the other hand, those who do follow Jesus will acquire a new family. "Jesus said, 'Amen, I say to you, there is no one who has given up house or brothers or sisters or mother or father or children or lands for my sake and for the sake of the gospel who will not receive a hundred times more now in this present age: houses and brothers and sisters and mothers and children and lands, with persecutions, and eternal life in the age to come'" (Mark 10:29-30).

This, ultimately, is why we today venerate Mary, because she sets the example of someone hearing the word of God and acting on it. Mary received the word of God from the angel Gabriel and was willing to let that word alter any plans or hopes she might have had concerning what her life was to be. From the moment she told Gabriel, "Behold, I am the handmaid of the Lord. May it be done to me according to your word" (Luke 1:38), her life fully belonged to whatever God and her son would make of it.

It is the Gospel of John that clears up any uncertainty about Mary's place in the new family Jesus was bringing about. Recalling what was said in the fifth sorrowful mystery, the crucifixion, just before he died, Jesus told Mary to behold the Beloved Disciple as her son and told the Beloved Disciple to behold Mary as his mother:

> When Jesus saw his mother and the disciple there whom he loved, he said to his mother, "Woman, behold, your son." Then he said to the disciple, "Behold, your mother." And from that hour the disciple took her into his home. (John 19:26-27)

Through his triumphant work on the cross, Jesus brought about a new family. This family is "new" in the most radical sense. Jesus has brought about a new creation, a new humanity. Scholars even notice allusions to the creation account in Genesis 2 in John's crucifixion scene. Having created a new human family in Mary and the Beloved Disciple, Jesus takes sour wine from a sponge brought to him on a hyssop branch, proclaims "It is finished," and "handed over the spirit" (John 19:29-30). As stated earlier, the spirit he handed over is understood as a symbolic gesture of what he will literally do on Easter Sunday, in the Upper Room: "[Jesus] said to them again, 'Peace be with you. As the Father has sent me, so I send you.' And when he had said this, he breathed on them and said to them, 'Receive the holy Spirit'" (John 20:21-22). Jesus' breath is the Holy Spirit, but it is also the creative breath of God, and just as God breathed life into the first human's nostrils, so the human family of the new creation is given the breath of God to be their ongoing source of life.

What does all this say about Mary's coronation? Nothing, directly, but everything in terms of the development of Christian doctrine. First fully expounded by John Henry Newman in 1845 (he was named a cardinal in 1879 by Pope Leo XIII, and beatified by Pope Benedict XVI in 2010), the central idea behind the development of Christian doctrine is that as the church ponders the gospel communicated to it in its fullness from the apostles, it discovers significant insights into the gospel that can and do lead to new understandings and conclusions about the content of the faith. What was not clearly understood in earlier times can be asserted with certainty and specificity later as the church learns to recognize new ramifications to the gospel, which was given once and for all to the church through apostolic teaching.

Scripture clearly proclaims to us Mary's role in bringing the Savior into the world and of her faithfulness as a disciple of her son. Beginning in its earliest days and deepening through time, trust in the communion of the saints and confidence in Mary's powerful intercession on behalf of a sinful humanity led the simplest souls and the wisest theologians to ponder what it meant that Mary was most highly favored by God and blessed among women. This is what eventually led to a number of beliefs not found directly in Scripture. Our belief in the immaculate conception and in her assumption into heaven, where she is "crowned" as the greatest of saints, is a development in faith springing from a faithful resonance with what Scripture does tell us about Mary. Filled with that faith in church teaching and confidence in the intercession of the Blessed Virgin Mary, we rejoice that we can ask for her assistance in leading us always to her Son, Jesus Christ our Lord.

Hail, Mary, full of grace, the Lord is with you;
blessed are you among women,
and blessed is the fruit of your womb, Jesus.
Holy Mary, Mother of God,
pray for us sinners
now and at the hour of our death.
Amen.

# Appendix A
## Annunciation and Nativity: Comparing Matthew and Luke

| | Annunciation | | | | Nativity | | | |
|---|---|---|---|---|---|---|---|---|
| | To whom | By whom | Context | Message | Instruction | Birthplace | Visitors | Animals? | Journeys |
| **Matthew** | Joseph (1:20) | An angel (1:20) | In a dream (1:20) By implication in Joseph's home in Bethlehem (no mention of a home in Nazareth until they return from Egypt, 2:19-23) | Mary is with child through the Holy Spirit (1:20) | Joseph is to name him "Jesus" for he will save his people, and he will be called Emmanuel (God with us, 1:21-23) | Bethlehem (no mention of an inn or manger, 2:4-9) | Magi, guided by a star (2:1-12) | None mentioned | After the birth from Bethlehem the Holy Family flee to Egypt (2:13-15) and eventually to Nazareth (2:19-23, Joseph takes them to Nazareth out of fear of Archelaus) |
| **Luke** | Mary (1:26-32) | The angel Gabriel (1:26) | Gabriel appears to Mary in Nazareth (1:26) | The Holy Spirit and the power of the Most High overshadow Mary (1:35) | Mary is to name him "Jesus." He will be called Son of the Most High (1:31-32) | In a manger in Bethlehem, for there was no room in the inn (2:7) | Shepherds, after being informed by angels where to find him (2:15-20) | None mentioned | From Nazareth to Bethlehem before the birth, then a return to Nazareth (2:1-4; 22; 39) |

*(columns: To whom, By whom, Context, Message are under "Annunciation"; Instruction, Birthplace, Visitors, Animals?, Journeys are under "Nativity")*

## Appendix B
The Complete Mysteries

### The Joyful Mysteries

1. The Annunciation
2. The Visitation
3. The Nativity
4. The Presentation
5. Finding the Young Jesus in the Temple

### The Mysteries of Light/Luminous Mysteries

1. The Baptism of the Lord
2. The Wedding at Cana
3. The Proclamation of the Kingdom of God
4. The Transfiguration
5. The Institution of the Eucharist

### The Sorrowful Mysteries

1. The Agony in the Garden
2. The Scourging at the Pillar
3. The Crowning with Thorns
4. Jesus Carries His Cross
5. The Crucifixion

### The Glorious Mysteries

1. The Resurrection
2. The Ascension
3. The Descent of the Holy Spirit
4. The Assumption of Mary
5. The Crowning of the Blessed Virgin as Queen of Heaven and Earth